Betty Crocker's Cooking for Two

Fresh, Flavorful Recipes for
Everyday and Special Occasions

italian kabobs (page 76)

Betty Crocker's Cooking for Two

Fresh, Flavorful Recipes for Everyday and Special Occasions

Hungry Minds

Best-Selling Books • Digital Downloads • e-Books • Answer Networks • e-Newsletters • Branded Web Sites • e-Learning

New York, NY • Cleveland, OH • Indianapolis, IN

Hungry Minds

Published by
Hungry Minds, Inc.
909 Third Avenue
New York, NY 10022
www.hungryminds.com

For general information on Hungry Minds' products and services please contact our Customer Care Department within the U.S. at 800-762-2974, outside the U.S. at 317-572-3993 or fax 317-572-4002.

For sales inquiries and reseller information, including discounts, premium and bulk quantity sales, and foreign-language translations, please contact our Customer Care Department at 800-434-3422, fax 317-572-4002, or write to Hungry Minds, Inc., Attn: Customer Care Department, 10475 Crosspoint Boulevard, Indianapolis, IN 46256.

Library of Congress Cataloging-in-Publication Data
Crocker, Betty.
    Betty Crocker's cooking for two : fresh, flavorful recipes for everyday and special occasions / Betty Crocker.
        p. cm.
    Rev. ed. of: Betty Crocker's new choices for two. 1995.
    Includes index.
    ISBN 0-7645-6108-1 (alk. paper)
    1. Cookery for two. I. Title: Cooking for two. II. Crocker, Betty. Betty Crocker's new choices for two.
III. Title.
TX652.C8318 2002
641.5'61—dc21   2001051477

GENERAL MILLS, INC.
Betty Crocker Kitchens
Manager, Publishing: Lois L. Tlusty
Recipe Development: Betty Crocker Kitchens Home Economists
Food Stylists: Betty Crocker Kitchens Food Stylists

Photographic Services
Photography: Photographic Services Department

HUNGRY MINDS, INC.
Cover Design: Michael Freeland
Interior Design: Holly Wittenberg
Editor: Caroline Schleifer

For consistent baking results, the Betty Crocker Kitchens recommend Gold Medal Flour.

For more great ideas visit **www.bettycrocker.com**

Manufactured in the United States of America
10 9 8 7 6 5 4 3 2 1

Cover photograph by David Bishop
Cover photos: Cheesy Asparagus Frittata (page 110) and Mango–Lime Cooler (page 174)

dear friends,

What do couples, newlyweds, roommates, "empty nesters" and single parents with a child have in common? Like so many households today, they're made up of twosomes. If you cook for two, you know it can be quite a challenge. This is the book that makes it easy and fun!

Here are more than 125 recipes perfectly tailored to make just the right quantities for any twosome. Choose a tasty entrée like Chicken Amandine (page 51), add a simple side like Roasted Fall Vegetables (page 145) and follow with a dessert such as Honey-Spice Apple (page 164). Voilà! A delicious meal for two is ready.

On days when things are a little more hectic, turn to the "On-the-Go Favorites" chapter for some great soup, sandwich or salad ideas. You can choose a recipe like Dilled Salmon Salad (page 22) or, if time permits, make two recipes, like Chicken and Cheese–Tortellini Soup (page 16) and Sweet Pepper Focaccia (page 39) for a quick, tasty meal.

You'll find "Good 2 Know" tips with every recipe, which give you helpful ideas on easy accompaniments, special touches, ingredient substitutions and more. Each chapter begins with "Solutions for 2," chockfull of good ideas ranging from super sandwiches to desserts that are so easy you won't even need to look up a recipe. Throughout, look for "Table for 2" for entertaining ideas that celebrate the fun of cooking for two. Need some ideas for Thanksgiving for the two of you? Turn to page 54 for some creative menu suggestions.

With *Betty Crocker's Cooking for Two*, you'll have a great time cooking—and enjoying—wonderful meals with the special person in your life.

Betty Crocker

PS: This cookbook should fit you to a "T"—Totally Terrific for Two!

apple crisp (page 165)

contents

solutions for 2

mix 'n' match salad sandwiches

Sandwiches are the ultimate on-the-go meal: they're easy to make for two as well as portable and delicious. Here's a chart that gives you plenty of ideas for sensational new sandwich combinations.

To savor all the possibilities, just stir together ingredients from each of the first three columns and fill the bread of your choice. Each combination makes two sandwiches.

Main Item (about 3/4 cup)	Dressings (about 1/4 cup)	Stir-Ins (choose 1 or 2)	Breads (choose enough for 2 sandwiches)
Chopped cooked roasted chicken or turkey	Mayonnaise or salad dressing	1/4 cup chopped celery, bell pepper, seedless cucumber or tomatoes	1 bagel, split
Chopped smoked turkey or ham	Plain or flavored whipped cream cheese	1/4 cup chopped apple, pear or water chestnuts	1 large pita bread, halved
Chopped roast beef	Dijon mayonnaise blend or creamy horseradish sauce	1/4 cup shredded Cheddar, Monterey Jack or mozzarella cheese	2 large plain or flavored flour tortillas
Chopped pastrami or corned beef	Sour cream or plain yogurt	2 tablespoons sliced green onions, chopped ripe or pimiento-stuffed olives or green chilies	2 hard, onion or kaiser rolls, split
3 hard-cooked eggs, chopped	Creamy bottled salad dressings such as Italian, Parmesan, ranch, blue cheese or peppercorn	2 tablespoons raisins, dried cranberries, chopped dried apricots or chopped nuts	2 English muffins or hamburger buns, split
Canned tuna, salmon or shrimp (4 to 6 ounces), drained	Creamy dips such as sour cream-and-onion, dill, avocado	2 slices crisply cooked bacon, crumbled	4 slices French bread, 1/2 inch thick, or sliced raisin, whole wheat or pumpernickel bread

on-the-go favorites

soups, salads, pizzas, sandwiches and more

hearty lentil soup

good 2 know A smoked Polish sausage like kielbasa gives this soup a great flavor. Salami and ham are good substitutes, though they don't have quite as much smokiness.

prep 10 min • **cook** 45 min

2 cups chicken broth

1 can or bottle (12 ounces) beer or 1 1/2 cups chicken broth

1/2 cup dried lentils, sorted and rinsed

1 medium carrot, sliced (about 1/2 cup)

1 medium stalk celery, chopped (1/2 cup)

1 small onion, chopped (1/4 cup)

1 fully cooked smoked Polish sausage (about 5 inches long), thinly sliced (about 3 ounces)

1 tablespoon chopped fresh or 1 teaspoon dried basil leaves

1/8 teaspoon pepper

1 small bay leaf

2 tablespoons grated Parmesan cheese

1. Heat broth, beer and lentils to boiling in 2-quart saucepan; reduce heat. Cover and simmer 20 to 25 minutes, stirring occasionally, until lentils are tender but not mushy.

2. Stir in remaining ingredients except cheese. Heat to boiling; reduce heat. Cover and simmer 20 minutes, stirring occasionally.

3. Remove bay leaf. Sprinkle each serving with cheese.

1 Serving: Calories 400 (Calories from Fat 135); Fat 20g (Saturated 6g); Cholesterol 30mg; Sodium 1590mg; Carbohydrate 42g (Dietary Fiber 13g); Protein 26g • **% Daily Value:** Vitamin A 100%; Vitamin C 6%; Calcium 16%; Iron 32% • **Diet Exchanges:** 2 Starch, 2 High-Fat Meat, 2 Vegetable

hearty lentil soup; curry chicken sandwiches (page 26)

cold gazpacho soup

There's nothing more refreshing than ice-cold gazpacho on a hot summer evening! If you have the time, chill the soup for about 30 minutes before serving in order to blend the flavors.

prep 12 min

1 cup tomato juice

2 tablespoons red wine vinegar

1/4 teaspoon sugar

1/4 teaspoon salt

Dash of Worcestershire sauce

2 medium tomatoes, chopped (1 1/2 cups)

1/2 cucumber, peeled and chopped (3/4 cup)

1/2 green bell pepper, chopped (1/2 cup)

2 tablespoons chopped onion

1 clove garlic, finely chopped

Chopped cilantro, if desired

1. Place all ingredients except cilantro in blender. Cover and blend at medium-high speed until blended but still chunky, stopping blender occasionally to scrape sides.

2. Pour into bowls; top with cilantro.

1 Serving: Calories 75 (Calories from Fat 10); Fat 1g (Saturated 0g); Cholesterol 0mg; Sodium 700mg; Carbohydrate 16g (Dietary Fiber 3g); Protein 3g • **% Daily Value:** Vitamin A 38%; Vitamin C 100%; Calcium 2%; Iron 8% • **Diet Exchanges:** 3 Vegetable

black bean soup

good2know   If you don't have tequila on hand you can flavor this rich-tasting soup with dry sherry instead, or leave it out altogether.

prep 15 min • **cook** 1 hr 5 min

1 can (14 1/2 ounces) chicken or vegetable broth

1 can (15 ounces) black beans, rinsed and drained

1 teaspoon chili powder

1/2 teaspoon ground cumin

1/8 teaspoon crushed red pepper

1 clove garlic, finely chopped

1 jalapeño chili, finely chopped

1 medium onion, chopped (1/2 cup)

1 small carrot, sliced (1/4 cup)

2 tablespoons tequila, if desired

1/4 cup diced jicama

2 tablespoons shredded Cheddar cheese

1 small tomato, seeded and chopped

1. Heat all ingredients except jicama, cheese and tomato to boiling; reduce heat. Cover and simmer 1 hour.

2. Carefully place about half the soup in blender or food processor. (Don't blend all the soup at once because steam can build up and cause the lid to come off.) Cover and blend at medium-high speed until smooth, stopping blender occasionally to scrape sides, until smooth. Pour into serving bowl; repeat with remaining bean mixture.

3. Serve topped with jicama, cheese and tomato.

1 Serving: Calories 355 (Calories from Fat 45); Fat 5g (Saturated 2g); Cholesterol 5mg; Sodium 1800mg; Carbohydrate 68g (Dietary Fiber 14g); Protein 26g • **% Daily Value:** Vitamin A 100%; Vitamin C 18%; Calcium 23%; Iron 34% • **Diet Exchanges:** 4 Starch, 1 Very Lean Meat, 1 Vegetable

vegetarian chili

good 2 know

There are so many ways to dress up this tasty chili. You can dollop it with sour cream or yogurt and add chopped avocados and fresh cilantro. Then serve a hearty roll or corn bread on the side.

prep 12 min • **cook** 25 min

1 teaspoon vegetable oil

1 medium onion, chopped (1/2 cup)

1/4 cup chopped green bell pepper

1 small zucchini, cut into 1 × 1/4 × 1/4-inch sticks (1 cup)

1 clove garlic, chopped

1 can (15 to 16 ounces) pinto beans, rinsed and drained

1 can (14 1/2 ounces) salsa tomatoes with diced green chilies, undrained

1 teaspoon chili powder

Sour cream, if desired

Chili powder, if desired

1. Heat oil in 2-quart nonstick saucepan over medium-high heat. Sauté onion, bell pepper, zucchini and garlic in oil. Stir in beans, tomatoes and chili powder.

2. Cover and cook over low heat 20 minutes. Serve with sour cream, sprinkle with chili powder.

1 Serving: Calories 380 (Calories from Fat 35); Fat 4g (Saturated 1g); Cholesterol 0mg; Sodium 940mg; Carbohydrate 76g (Dietary Fiber 22g); Protein 21g • **% Daily Value:** Vitamin A 22%; Vitamin C 48%; Calcium 18%; Iron 38% • **Diet Exchanges:** 4 Starch, 3 Vegetable

vegetarian chili

chicken and cheese-tortellini soup

Enjoy this hearty soup as a main course for lunch or for a light supper. Looking for ways to eat more vegetables? Stir in fresh or frozen greens like spinach along with the tortellini.

prep 8 min • **cook** 25 min

2 boneless, skinless chicken breast halves (about 1/2 pound)

1 medium carrot, sliced (1/2 cup)

2 to 3 medium green onions, sliced (1/4 cup)

1/2 cup cubed parsnip

3 cups chicken broth

1 teaspoon chopped fresh or 1/4 teaspoon dried marjoram leaves

3 ounces uncooked refrigerated or frozen (thawed) cheese-filled tortellini (about 1/2 cup)

2 tablespoons grated Parmesan cheese

1. Cut chicken into 1-inch pieces. Heat chicken, carrot, onions, parsnip, broth and marjoram to boiling in 2-quart saucepan; reduce heat.

2. Cover and simmer about 15 minutes, stirring occasionally, until chicken is no longer pink in center and vegetables are almost tender.

3. Stir in tortellini. Heat to boiling; reduce heat. Simmer uncovered about 5 minutes, stirring occasionally, until tortellini are tender. Sprinkle with cheese.

1 Serving: Calories 325 (Calories from Fat 100); Fat 11g (Saturated 4g); Cholesterol 110mg; Sodium 1780mg; Carbohydrate 20g (Dietary Fiber 3g); Protein 39g • **% Daily Value:** Vitamin A 100%; Vitamin C 8%; Calcium 18%; Iron 14% • **Diet Exchanges:** 1 Starch, 5 Very Lean Meat, 1 Vegetable, 1 Fat

tarragon fish chowder

good 2 know Tarragon adds a mild hint of licorice to this comforting chowder. If you don't have any on hand, use parsley instead.

prep 10 min • cook 10 min

1/2 pound cod or other
lean fish fillets

1 1/2 cups chicken broth

1 small onion, chopped
(1/4 cup)

1/4 cup sliced celery

1/4 cup shredded carrot

3/4 teaspoon chopped fresh
or 1/4 teaspoon dried
tarragon leaves

1/8 teaspoon pepper

1 bay leaf

1 cup milk

1/2 cup sour cream

1 tablespoon all-purpose flour

1. Cut fish fillets into bite-size pieces. Mix fish, broth, onion, celery, carrot, tarragon, pepper and bay leaf in 1 1/2-quart saucepan. Heat to boiling; reduce heat.

2. Cover and simmer 2 to 3 minutes or until fish flakes easily with fork and vegetables are tender. Stir in milk; heat through.

3. Mix sour cream and flour; stir into milk mixture. Cook, stirring constantly, just until mixture starts to bubble (do not boil). Immediately remove from heat; remove bay leaf.

tablefor2 For a cozy winter meal in front of the fireplace, serve this rich chowder with a crisp tossed salad and crusty French bread.

1 Serving: Calories 335 (Calories from Fat 145); Fat 16g (Saturated 9g); Cholesterol 110mg; Sodium 960mg; Carbohydrate 17g (Dietary Fiber 1g); Protein 32g • **% Daily Value:** Vitamin A 64%; Vitamin C 4%; Calcium 24%; Iron 6% • **Diet Exchanges:** 3 1/2 Lean Meat, 2 Vegetable, 1/2 Skim Milk, 1 Fat

cheese and ham tabbouleh salad

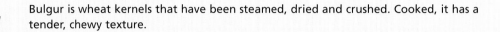 **good 2 know** Bulgur is wheat kernels that have been steamed, dried and crushed. Cooked, it has a tender, chewy texture.

prep 35 min • **chill** 4 hr

1/2 cup uncooked bulgur

1 medium tomato, chopped (3/4 cup)

1/2 cup chopped seeded cucumber

1/2 cup cubed Swiss cheese (2 ounces)

1/4 cup diced fully cooked smoked ham

1/4 cup chopped fresh parsley

2 tablespoons thinly sliced green onions

1 tablespoon chopped fresh or 1 teaspoon crushed dried mint leaves

3 tablespoons olive or vegetable oil

3 tablespoons lemon juice

1/8 teaspoon salt

1/8 teaspoon pepper

Lettuce leaves, if desired

1. Cover bulgur with cold water in bowl. Let stand 30 minutes; drain. Press out as much water as possible.

2. Place bulgur, tomato, cucumber, cheese, ham, parsley and onions in glass or plastic bowl. Mix remaining ingredients except lettuce leaves; pour over bulgur mixture and toss.

3. Cover and refrigerate at least 4 hours or overnight. Serve bulgur mixture on lettuce leaves.

1 Serving: Calories 470 (Calories from Fat 290); Fat 32g (Saturated 9g); Cholesterol 40mg; Sodium 510g; Carbohydrate 34g (Dietary Fiber 8g); Protein 19g • **% Daily Value:** Vitamin A 32%; Vitamin C 50%; Calcium 36%; Iron 12% • **Diet Exchanges:** 2 Starch, 1 1/2 High-Fat Meat, 1 Vegetable, 3 Fat

cheese and ham tabbouleh salad

zucchini-couscous salad

This salad makes a great light lunch or side dish. For a more substantial main course salad, add grilled chicken or shrimp.

prep 15 min • **chill** 1 hr • *photograph on page 79*

1/2 cup chicken broth

1/4 cup uncooked couscous

1/2 zucchini, shredded

1/4 cup chopped green, red or yellow bell pepper

2 tablespoons white vinegar or white wine vinegar

1 tablespoon vegetable oil

1 teaspoon chopped fresh or 1/4 teaspoon dried savory leaves

1 teaspoon sesame oil

1/2 teaspoon sugar

Lettuce leaves, if desired

1. Heat broth to boiling in 1-quart saucepan; remove from heat. Stir in couscous. Cover and let stand 5 minutes.

2. Mix couscous, zucchini and bell pepper in medium glass or plastic bowl. Shake remaining ingredients except lettuce leaves in tightly covered container. Pour over couscous mixture; stir to coat.

3. Cover and refrigerate at least 1 hour. Serve on lettuce leaves.

1 Serving: Calories 180 (Calories from Fat 80); Fat 9g (Saturated 1g); Cholesterol 0mg; Sodium 260mg; Carbohydrate 21g (Dietary Fiber 2g); Protein 5g • **% Daily Value:** Vitamin A 6%; Vitamin C 30%; Calcium 0%; Iron 4% • **Diet Exchanges:** 1 Starch, 1 Vegetable, 1 1/2 Fat

santa fe turkey salad

Serve this irresistible Southwestern salad with some crunchy tortilla chips on the side, and add a slice of lime to your favorite beverage.

prep 15 min

1 cup cut-up cooked turkey

2 tablespoons sour cream

2 tablespoons mayonnaise
or salad dressing

2 tablespoons chopped onion

2 tablespoons finely chopped
fresh cilantro

1 tablespoon lime juice

1 tablespoon capers

1 tablespoon diced pimientos

1/4 teaspoon ground cumin

1 teaspoon chopped fresh
or 1/4 teaspoon dried
oregano leaves

Lettuce leaves

1/4 avocado, cut into wedges

Paprika, if desired

1. Toss all ingredients except lettuce, avocado and paprika.

2. Serve salad on lettuce. Garnish with avocado. Sprinkle with paprika.

1 Serving: Calories 300 (Calories from Fat 200); Fat 22g (Saturated 5g); Cholesterol 80mg; Sodium 260mg; Carbohydrate 5g (Dietary Fiber 1g); Protein 21g • **% Daily Value:** Vitamin A 10%; Vitamin C 18%; Calcium 2%; Iron 6% • **Diet Exchanges:** 3 Medium-Fat Meat, 1 Vegetable, 1 Fat

dilled salmon salad

prep 10 min • cook 10 min • chill 2 hr

1/2 pound salmon steaks

2 cups chicken broth

1 small zucchini, sliced (1 cup)

1/4 cup sliced radishes

1/4 cup mayonnaise or salad dressing

2 tablespoons ranch dressing

1 teaspoon chopped fresh or 1/4 teaspoon dried dill weed

3 cups bite-size pieces spinach or other salad greens

1. Place fish steaks and broth in 10-inch skillet. Heat to boiling; reduce heat. Simmer uncovered 5 to 10 minutes or until fish flakes easily with fork. Remove fish to platter. When fish is cool enough to handle, break into bite-size pieces, discarding skin and bones.

2. Mix salmon, zucchini and radishes in large bowl. Mix mayonnaise, ranch dressing and dill weed; fold into salmon mixture.

3. Cover and refrigerate at least 2 hours. Serve salmon mixture on spinach or toss before serving.

1 Serving: Calories 430 (Calories from Fat 315); Fat 35g (Saturated 6g); Cholesterol 85mg; Sodium 660mg; Carbohydrate 6g (Dietary Fiber 2g); Protein 25g • **% Daily Value:** Vitamin A 94%; Vitamin C 38%; Calcium 10%; Iron 14% • **Diet Exchanges:** 3 High-Fat Meat, 1 Vegetable, 2 Fat

chicken fruit salad

This light and fruity salad tastes best in summer when peaches or nectarines are at their peak. Serve it on lettuce leaves for salad or stuff it into a pita half for a terrific sandwich.

prep 10 min • **chill** 30 min

1/3 cup plain low-fat yogurt

2 tablespoons mayonnaise or salad dressing

1 cup cubed cooked chicken breast

2/3 cup seedless green grapes

1 large peach, chopped (3/4 cup)

1 medium stalk celery, diced (1/2 cup)

1 teaspoon chopped fresh or 1/2 teaspoon dried mint leaves

1. Mix yogurt and mayonnaise in medium bowl until smooth. Stir in remaining ingredients.

2. Cover and refrigerate at least 30 minutes or until chilled.

1 Serving: Calories 310 (Calories from Fat 135); Fat 15g (Saturated 3g); Cholesterol 70mg; Sodium 180mg; Carbohydrate 22g (Dietary Fiber 0g); Protein 34g • **% Daily Value:** Vitamin A 4%; Vitamin C 20%; Calcium 10%; Iron 6% • **Diet Exchanges:** 3 1/2 Lean Meat, 1 1/2 Fruit, 1 Fat

apple-cheese melts

With Gorgonzola cheese, the saying "a little goes a long way" is especially apt! It's a strong but delicious creamy blue cheese.

prep 5 min • **broil** 5 min

2 slices French or Italian bread, each 1-inch thick

2 tablespoons applesauce

1 medium apple, cored and cut into rings

2 ounces Cheddar cheese, sliced

2 ounces Gorgonzola cheese, crumbled

1. Set oven control to broil. Place bread on ungreased cookie sheet. Broil with tops about 4 inches from heat until golden brown; turn.

2. Spread applesauce on bread slices. Place half of apple rings on each bread slice. Top with cheeses. Broil just until cheese begins to melt.

1 Serving: Calories 350 (Calories from Fat 170); Fat 19g (Saturated 12g); Cholesterol 50mg; Sodium 780mg; Carbohydrate 32g (Dietary Fiber 3g); Protein 16g • **% Daily Value:** Vitamin A 10%; Vitamin C 2%; Calcium 32%; Iron 8% • **Diet Exchanges:** 1 Starch, 2 High-Fat Meat, 1 Fruit

apple-cheese melts

curry chicken sandwiches

good 2 know When purchasing buns for these sandwiches, consider individual ones from the super-market bakery. That way, you have just the right amount! Hearty lentil soup makes a great soup 'n' sandwich dinner combo.

prep 5 min • **broil** 9 min • *photograph on page 11*

1 tablespoon butter or margarine, melted

1/4 teaspoon lemon pepper

2 boneless, skinless chicken breast halves (about 1/2 pound)

Salt

Pepper

1 tablespoon mayonnaise or salad dressing

1 tablespoon plain yogurt or sour cream

1/4 teaspoon curry powder

2 lettuce leaves

2 kaiser rolls or hamburger buns, split

1. Set oven control to broil.

2. Mix butter and lemon pepper. Brush chicken breast halves with half of the butter mixture. Place chicken on rack in broiler pan. Broil with tops 4 inches from heat about 4 minutes or until chicken just starts to brown. Sprinkle lightly with salt and pepper. Turn chicken; brush with remaining butter mixture. Broil about 5 minutes longer or until chicken is brown on outside and juices are no longer pink when center of thickest piece is cut.

3. Meanwhile, mix mayonnaise, yogurt and curry powder. Place lettuce leaf on bottom of each roll. Place chicken on lettuce. Top with dollop of mayonnaise mixture and top of roll.

1 Serving: Calories 385 (Calories from Fat 155); Fat 17g (Saturated 6g); Cholesterol 95mg; Sodium 1010mg; Carbohydrate 27g (Dietary Fiber 1g); Protein 32g • **% Daily Value:** Vitamin A 10%; Vitamin C 2%; Calcium 8%; Iron 14% • **Diet Exchanges:** 2 Starch, 3 1/2 Lean Meat, 1 Fat

blue cheese quesadillas

These quesadillas are great served with a fruity salsa like the one for Caribbean Swordfish (page 65). If you don't have time to prepare your own salsa, try it with tangy mango chutney instead.

prep 5 min • **bake** 10 min

1/2 cup shredded Monterey Jack cheese (2 ounces)

1/4 cup soft-style cream cheese

3 tablespoons chopped walnuts

2 tablespoons crumbled blue cheese

1 green onion, sliced

4 flour tortillas (6 inches in diameter)

Fruit salsa or chutney, if desired

1. Heat oven to 375°. Grease cookie sheet.

2. Mix all ingredients except tortillas and salsa. Place two tortillas on cookie sheet and spread with cheese mixture. Top with remaining tortillas. Bake 8 to 10 minutes or until cheese begins to melt and tortillas start to brown.

3. Cut into wedges and serve with salsa.

1 Serving: Calories 430 (Calories from Fat 250); Fat 28g (Saturated 13g); Cholesterol 55mg; Sodium 590mg; Carbohydrate 30g (Dietary Fiber 2g); Protein 16g • **% Daily Value:** Vitamin A 14%; Vitamin C 0%; Calcium 34%; Iron 12% • **Diet Exchanges:** 2 Starch, 2 High-Fat Meat, 2 1/2 Fat

crab-dijon sandwiches

good 2 know
Here's a grown-up take on the tuna melt that's just as delicious. Serve it with tomato soup for a light lunch or try it with Cold Gazpacho Soup (page 12) to beat the summer heat.

prep 3 min • broil 4 min

6 ounces frozen crabmeat or frozen salad-style imitation crabmeat, thawed

1/4 cup mayonnaise or salad dressing

2 tablespoons grated Parmesan cheese

1 teaspoon Dijon mustard

2 English muffins, split and toasted

1. Set oven control to broil.

2. Mix crabmeat, mayonnaise, cheese and mustard. Divide among muffin halves. Place on rack in broiler pan. Broil with tops 4 inches from heat 3 to 4 minutes or until tops start to brown.

1 Serving: Calories 445 (Calories from Fat 245); Fat 27g (Saturated 5g); Cholesterol 105mg; Sodium 960mg; Carbohydrate 28g (Dietary Fiber 2g); Protein 25g • **% Daily Value:** Vitamin A 2%; Vitamin C 4%; Calcium 28%; Iron 14% • **Diet Exchanges:** 2 Starch, 3 Lean Meat, 3 Fat

zesty barbecue sandwiches

good2know Serve these sandwiches with baked beans and coleslaw and you can have a down-home "barbecue" any time of year!

cook 10 min

1/2 cup ketchup

1 tablespoon orange marmalade

1/2 teaspoon chili powder

6 ounces thinly sliced cooked roast beef or pork

2 kaiser rolls or hamburger buns, split and toasted

1. Mix ketchup, orange marmalade and chili powder in 1-quart saucepan. Cover and cook over low heat 5 minutes, stirring occasionally.

2. Stir in roast beef. Cover and cook over low heat 5 minutes, stirring occasionally. Fill rolls with beef mixture.

1 Serving: Calories 440 (Calories from Fat 135); Fat 15g (Saturated 5g); Cholesterol 70mg; Sodium 1040mg; Carbohydrate 49g (Dietary Fiber 2g); Protein 29g • **% Daily Value:** Vitamin A 16%; Vitamin C 8%; Calcium 6%; Iron 24% • **Diet Exchanges:** 3 Starch, 3 Lean Meat, 1 Fat

caesar salad wraps

good 2 know   In this special twist on the classic favorite, here's a salad and sandwich in one. For a tasty variation, you can stir about 1 cup of cut-up cooked chicken into the romaine filling mixture.

prep 15 min

8 small romaine leaves

2 tablespoons chopped red onion

1 tablespoon shredded Parmesan or Romano cheese

2 tablespoons Caesar dressing

2 garden vegetable–flavored flour tortillas (6 or 8 inches in diameter)

2 hard-cooked eggs, sliced

1 roma (plum) tomato, sliced

1. Toss romaine, onion, cheese and dressing to coat.

2. Place romaine mixture evenly down center of each tortilla. Top with eggs and tomato.

3. Fold up one end of tortilla about 1 inch over filling; fold right and left sides over folded end, overlapping. Fold remaining end down; secure with toothpick if necessary.

1 Serving: Calories 285 (Calories from Fat 135); Fat 15g (Saturated 4g); Cholesterol 220mg; Sodium 470mg; Carbohydrate 27g (Dietary Fiber 2g); Protein 12g • **% Daily Value:** Vitamin A 16%; Vitamin C 14%; Calcium 14%; Iron 12% • **Diet Exchanges:** 1 1/2 Starch, 1 High-Fat Meat, 1 Vegetable, 1 Fat

caesar salad wraps

turkey "cranwiches"

good 2 know There's no need to reserve this tasty sandwich with "all the fixings" for after Thanksgiving; it's delicious at any time of year.

prep 5 min • **cook** 7 min

2 slices (3/4 ounce each) Colby, Monterey Jack or Cheddar cheese, cut into halves

1/4 cup cranberry-orange sauce or relish

6 ounces thinly sliced cooked turkey

4 slices firm-textured wheat or rye bread

1 to 2 tablespoons butter or margarine, softened

1. Layer half each of the cheese, sauce and turkey on 2 slices bread. Top with remaining bread. Spread top slices of bread with about half of the butter.

2. Place sandwiches, butter side down, in 10-inch skillet. Spread top slices of bread with butter. Cook uncovered over medium heat about 5 minutes or until golden brown. Turn and cook about 2 minutes longer or until golden brown and cheese is melted.

1 Serving: Calories 410 (Calories from Fat 155); Fat 17g (Saturated 9g); Cholesterol 80mg; Sodium 1450mg; Carbohydrate 42g (Dietary Fiber 3g); Protein 25g • **% Daily Value:** Vitamin A 8%; Vitamin C 4%; Calcium 16%; Iron 12% • **Diet Exchanges:** 2 Starch, 3 Lean Meat, 1 Fruit,1 Fat

chicken salad croissant sandwiches

good 2 know   Here's a quick way to cook chicken for chopped chicken salad: use your microwave! The chicken steams in its own juices and comes out moist and tender.

prep 5 min • **microwave** 4 min • **chill** 30 min

2 boneless, skinless chicken breast halves (about 1/2 pound)

1/4 cup creamy ranch-style dressing

1/2 teaspoon yellow mustard

1/4 cup chopped cucumber

1/4 cup chopped tomato

2 tablespoons chopped cashews

2 croissants, cut lengthwise into halves

Butter, margarine, mayonnaise or salad dressing, if desired

1/2 cup alfalfa sprouts

1. Place chicken breast halves in 16-ounce casserole or on plate with thickest parts toward outside edges. Cover tightly and microwave on High (100%) until thickest parts are done, 3 to 4 minutes. Uncover and refrigerate until cool enough to handle, about 10 minutes.

2. Cut chicken into 1/4-inch pieces. Place chicken, dressing, mustard, cucumber, tomato and cashews in bowl; toss. Cover and refrigerate until chilled.

3. Just before serving, spread cut sides of croissant halves with butter. Spread chicken mixture over bottoms of croissants; top with alfalfa sprouts and the other croissant halves.

1 Serving: Calories 595 (Calories from Fat 335); Fat 37g (Saturated 12g); Cholesterol 140mg; Sodium 500mg; Carbohydrate 33g (Dietary Fiber 2g); Protein 34g • **% Daily Value:** Vitamin A 16%; Vitamin C 10%; Calcium 10%; Iron 16% • **Diet Exchanges:** 2 Starch, 4 Lean Meat, 1 Vegetable, 4 Fat

peppercorn beef pitas

good 2 know If you'd rather have turkey than roast beef, use cubed cooked turkey or smoked turkey from the deli. For a terrific salad, toss the filling ingredients together and serve the pita bread on the side.

prep 10 min

2 cups ready-to-eat romaine and leaf lettuce (half of 10-ounce bag)

1/4 pound cubed cooked roast beef (2/3 cup)

2 roma (plum) tomatoes, cut lengthwise in half and sliced

1/4 cup peppercorn ranch dressing

1 pita bread (8 inches in diameter), cut in half to form pockets

Sliced red onion, if desired

1. Toss lettuce, beef, tomatoes and dressing.

2. Spoon mixture evenly into pita bread halves. Top with onion.

1 Sandwich: Calories 405 (Calories from Fat 205); Fat 23g (Saturated 5g); Cholesterol 55mg; Sodium 580mg; Carbohydrate 31g (Dietary Fiber 3g); Protein 22g • **% Daily Value:** Vitamin A 32%; Vitamin C 38%; Calcium 10%; Iron 20% • **Diet Exchanges:** 2 Starch, 2 1/2 Lean Meat, 2 1/2 Fat

cheesy artichoke calzones

good 2 know A calzone is a stuffed pizza that looks like a big turnover. When you're short on time, just pick up prepared pizza dough in the refrigerator or freezer section of your supermarket.

prep 35 min • **rest** 5 min • **bake** 35 min

Pizza Crust (below)

1 jar (6 ounces) marinated artichoke hearts

1/2 cup shredded Cheddar cheese (2 ounces)

1/2 cup soft-style cream cheese with chives and onions

1/4 cup julienne strips or diced fully-cooked smoked ham

1 tablespoon fresh chopped or 1 teaspoon dried oregano leaves

1. Heat oven to 375°. Grease cookie sheet. Prepare crust.

2. Drain artichokes well, reserving 1 tablespoon marinade. Coarsely chop artichokes. Mix artichokes, reserved marinade and remaining ingredients.

3. Divide dough for crust into halves. Pat each half into an 8-inch circle on cookie sheet, using floured fingers. Spoon artichoke mixture onto half of each dough circle. Moisten edges of dough circles with water. Fold dough over filling. Seal edges by pressing with tines of fork.

4. Bake 30 to 35 minutes or until crust is golden brown.

pizza crust

1 package regular or quick-acting active dry yeast

1/2 cup warm water (105° to 115°)

1 1/4 cups all-purpose flour

1 tablespoon olive or vegetable oil

1/8 teaspoon salt

Dissolve yeast in warm water in medium bowl. Stir in remaining ingredients. Beat vigorously 20 strokes. Let rest 5 minutes. Knead in enough flour to make dough easy to handle.

1 Serving: Calories 670 (Calories from Fat 305); Fat 34g (Saturated 17g); Cholesterol 85mg; Sodium 930mg; Carbohydrate 72g (Dietary Fiber 7g); Protein 26g • **% Daily Value:** Vitamin A 18%; Vitamin C 6%; Calcium 22%; Iron 34% • **Diet Exchanges:** 4 Starch, 1 1/2 High-Fat Meat, 2 Vegetable, 3 1/2 Fat

middle eastern pita pizzas

This veggie pizza makes a great light meal. For meat lovers, sprinkle 1 or 2 tablespoons of chopped cooked chicken over the hummus for each pita.

prep 10 min • bake 10 min

2 pita breads (6 inches in diameter)

1/4 cup roasted garlic-flavored or regular hummus

1/2 cup crumbled feta cheese (2 ounces)

1/2 small onion, sliced

1 cup shredded spinach

1 medium tomato, seeded and chopped (1/2 cup)

2 tablespoons sliced ripe or kalamata olives

1. Heat oven to 400°. Place pita breads in ungreased jelly roll pan, 15 1/2 × 10 1/2 × 1 inch.

2. Spread hummus on each pita bread. Sprinkle with cheese.

3. Bake 8 to 10 minutes or until cheese is melted. Top each pizza with onion, spinach, tomato and olives.

1 Serving: Calories 290 (Calories from Fat 90); Fat 10g (Saturated Fat 5g); Cholesterol 25mg; Sodium 790mg; Carbohydrate 42g (Dietary Fiber 5g); Protein 13g • **% Daily Value:** Vitamin A 40%; Vitamin C 14%; Calcium 24%; Iron 20% • **Diet Exchanges:** 2 Starch, 1/2 Very Lean Meat, 2 Vegetables, 2 Fat

middle eastern pita pizzas

vegetarian pizza

Broccoli slaw is made of julienned strips of fresh broccoli stalks mixed with shredded red cabbage and carrot. Look for it near the coleslaw mix in the produce section.

prep 5 min • bake 10 min

1 package (8 ounces) ready-to-serve Italian pizza crusts (6 inches in diameter)

1/2 cup pizza sauce

1 cup broccoli slaw

1 cup sliced mushrooms

1/4 cup chopped green or red bell pepper

1 cup shredded Italian-style four-cheese combination or mozzarella cheese (4 ounces)

1. Heat oven to 400°. Grease cookie sheet.

2. Place pizza crusts on ungreased cookie sheet. Spread pizza sauce over crusts. Top with broccoli slaw, mushrooms and green pepper. Sprinkle with cheese. Bake 8 to 10 minutes or until pizza is hot and cheese is melted.

1 Serving: Calories 390(Calories from Fat 145); Fat 16g (Saturated 7g); Cholesterol 30mg; Sodium 880mg; Carbohydrate 42g (Dietary Fiber 4g); Protein 23g • **% Daily Value:** Vitamin A 46%; Vitamin C 74%; Calcium 46%; Iron 18% • **Diet Exchanges:** 2 Starch, 2 Medium-Fat Meat, 2 Vegetable

sweet pepper focaccia

good2know Focaccia is an Italian flatbread that looks like a bumpy pizza crust. A ready-to-serve pizza crust can be used instead. You can keep some in the freezer for quick lunches and easy snacks.

prep 7 min • **bake** 5 min

1 small focaccia crust (7 inches in diameter)

1 tablespoon low-fat Italian dressing

1 small green bell pepper, cut into rings

1 roma (plum) tomato, chopped (1/4 cup)

1 teaspoon grated Parmesan cheese

Fresh oregano leaves, chopped, if desired

1. Heat oven to 425°.

2. Place focaccia crust on ungreased cookie sheet; drizzle half of dressing evenly over crust. Top with bell pepper, tomato and cheese. Drizzle with remaining dressing.

3. Bake 5 minutes or until edge of crust is golden brown. Sprinkle with oregano.

1 Serving: Calories 305 (Calories from Fat 90); Fat 10g (Saturated 2g); Cholesterol 0mg; Sodium 880mg; Carbohydrate 49g (Dietary Fiber 3g); Protein 8g • **% Daily Value:** Vitamin A 6%; Vitamin C 32%; Calcium 2%; Iron 18% • **Diet Exchanges:** 3 Starch, 1 Vegetable, 1 Fat

three-cheese fondue

good 2 know

Fondue is French for "melted" and you can make one at home easily, even if you don't have a fondue set. Just take your time stirring in the cheeses, allowing each addition to completely melt into the wine before adding more.

prep 10 min • **cook** 15 min

1/2 cup shredded Swiss cheese (2 ounces)

1/2 cup shredded Colby cheese (2 ounces)

1/2 cup shredded Monterey Jack cheese (2 ounces)

2 teaspoons cornstarch

1 clove garlic, cut in half

1/2 cup dry white wine or nonalcoholic white wine

2 tablespoons dry sherry, kirsch or nonalcoholic white wine

1/4 teaspoon ground ginger

Several dashes of red pepper sauce

French bread, cut into 1-inch pieces, or vegetable dippers

1. Toss cheeses and cornstarch until cheese is coated.

2. Rub garlic on bottom and side of fondue pot, heavy 1-quart saucepan or skillet; discard garlic. Add wine. Heat over simmer setting or low heat just until bubbles rise to surface (do not boil).

3. Gradually add cheese mixture, about 1/4 cup at a time, stirring constantly with wooden spoon over low heat, until melted. Stir in sherry, ginger and pepper sauce.

4. Keep warm over simmer setting. If prepared in saucepan or skillet, pour into a fondue pot or heatproof serving bowl and keep warm over low heat.

5. Spear bread with fondue forks; dip and swirl in fondue with stirring motion. If fondue becomes too thick, stir in small amount of heated wine.

table for 2

Fondue, served with a tossed green salad, is a natural for a romantic candlelit dinner for two. And remember the fondue rule: A dropped dipper requires a kiss!

1 Serving Fondue: Calories 375 (Calories from Fat 235); Fat 26g (Saturated 16g); Cholesterol 80mg; Sodium 430mg; Carbohydrate 13g (Dietary Fiber 0g); Protein 22g • **% Daily Value:** Vitamin A 18%; Vitamin C 0%; Calcium 62%; Iron 2% • **Diet Exchanges:** 1 Starch, 3 High-Fat Meat
NOTE: Nutrition information is only for fondue—does not include any dippers or bread.

cheese enchiladas

Try these enchiladas, made with fat-free cottage cheese and reduced-fat cheese, for all the ooey-gooey cheesy deliciousness you expect—with much less fat!

prep 12 min • bake 20 min

1/2 cup fat-free cottage cheese

1/2 cup plus 1/4 cup shredded reduced-fat Monterey Jack or Cheddar cheese

1 small tomato, chopped (1/2 cup)

2 green onions, sliced

1 teaspoon chili powder

1/4 teaspoon salt

1 small clove garlic, finely chopped

4 corn tortillas (6 inches in diameter)

1/4 cup mild taco sauce

1. Heat oven to 375°. Spray two 14-ounce shallow oval casseroles or rectangular baking dish 11 × 7 × 1 1/2 inches, with cooking spray.

2. Mix cottage cheese, 1/2 cup Monterey Jack cheese, the tomato, onions, chili powder, salt and garlic. Spread about 1/3 cup of the cheese mixture on each tortilla. Roll up tortillas; place seam side down in casseroles. Spoon taco sauce over tortillas; sprinkle with 1/4 cup Monterey Jack cheese.

3. Bake uncovered 15 to 20 minutes or until hot and cheese is melted.

1 Serving: Calories 290 (Calories from Fat 80); Fat 9g (Saturated 5g); Cholesterol 25mg; Sodium 1050mg; Carbohydrate 32g (Dietary Fiber 4g); Protein 24g • **% Daily Value:** Vitamin A 24%; Vitamin C 12%; Calcium 52%; Iron 8% • **Diet Exchanges:** 1 1/2 Starch, 2 1/2 Lean Meat, 1 Vegetable

solutions for 2

stop 'n' shop

Shopping smart is the first step to cooking great meals. But sometimes it seems like everything in the supermarket comes super-sized, when all you need is enough for two. Here are some great ways to make shopping for two a breeze . . .

- **Make lists** of what you need to speed up your shopping. Lists are especially important to keep from buying too much!

- **Shop for the basics**, such as household goods, foods that will keep and bottled beverages at the supermarket, warehouse club or food cooperative. If you have a large freezer, you can purchase family-pack meats and poultry and individually freeze portions so you have them on hand.

- **Check out farmers markets**, natural-food stores, ethnic-food stores or your local grocery store— you may discover some new ingredients you like and you can often find foods that are sold in smaller quantities.

- **Try salad bars** that offer cut-up fresh vegetables and fruits for a great timesaver. They are also a great source if you just need a little bit of several ingredients for a stir-fry or other skillet meal. Check out the variety of salad dressings available there too!

- **Add flavor to foods** without a lot of extra ingredients with prepared foods such as salsas, chutneys, relishes and marinades. Select canned and bottled goods in small or individual sizes: while it may seem more expensive than buying larger sizes, it can save you money in the long run and will help prevent waste.

- **Select ground meat**, steaks or chops when you're cooking meat. They are the easiest cuts to cook for two. Enjoy roasts when you have guests, since they are best when at least two pounds of meat are cooked. Or cook a roast then freeze part of the leftovers.

- **Pick up a nice selection** of cold cuts and cheese in the deli section and bread or rolls in the bakery department on those days when you don't feel like cooking a full meal.

enjoyable entrées

chicken, fish and meat dishes

caesar chicken with orzo

Complete with chicken, pasta and vegetables, this all-in-one skillet meal needs no extras. For a special occasion, serve with warmed purchased focaccia and fresh pears or clusters of red grapes for dessert.

prep 5 min • **cook** 25 min

1 1/2 teaspoons vegetable oil

2 boneless, skinless chicken breast halves (about 1/2 pound)

1 cup chicken broth

1/2 cup water

1/2 cup uncooked rosamarina (orzo) pasta (3 ounces)

1/2 bag (1-pound size) frozen baby whole carrots, green beans and yellow beans

1 1/2 tablespoons Caesar dressing

1/8 teaspoon coarsely ground pepper

1. Heat oil in 10-inch skillet over medium-high heat. Cook chicken in oil about 10 minutes, turning once, until brown. Remove chicken from skillet; keep warm.

2. Add broth and water to skillet; heat to boiling. Stir in pasta; heat to boiling. Cook uncovered 8 to 10 minutes, stirring occasionally, until pasta is tender. Stir in frozen vegetables and dressing. Add chicken. Sprinkle with pepper.

3. Heat to boiling; reduce heat. Simmer uncovered about 5 minutes or until vegetables are crisp-tender and juice of chicken is no longer pink when center of thickest pieces are cut.

1 Serving: Calories 375 (Calories from Fat 115); Fat 13g (Saturated 3g); Cholesterol 75mg; Sodium 730mg; Carbohydrate 35g (Dietary Fiber 5g); Protein 35g • **% Daily Value:** Vitamin A 100%; Vitamin C 2%; Calcium 8%; Iron 18% • **Diet Exchanges:** 2 Starch, 4 Lean Meat, 1 Vegetable

caesar chicken with orzo

baked chicken and potato dinner

good2know This baked dish brings home all the flavors of roast chicken with vegetables. And cleanup is carefree if you line the baking dish with aluminum foil before spraying with cooking spray. Now cleanup means tossing out the foil!

prep 20 min • **bake** 40 min

2 boneless, skinless
chicken breast halves
(about 1/2 pound)

2 tablespoons Dijon mustard

1/2 cup Reduced Fat or
Original Bisquick®

3/4 pound small red potatoes,
cut into fourths

1 small red or green
bell pepper, cut into
1/2-inch pieces

1 small onion, cut into
8 wedges

Cooking spray

2 tablespoons grated
Parmesan cheese, if desired

1/2 teaspoon paprika

1. Heat oven to 400°. Spray baking dish, 13 × 9 × 2 inches, with cooking spray.

2. Brush chicken with 1 tablespoon of the mustard, then coat with Bisquick. Place 1 chicken breast half in each corner of pan. Place potatoes, bell pepper and onion in center of pan; brush vegetables with remaining mustard. Spray chicken and vegetables with cooking spray; sprinkle evenly with cheese and paprika.

3. Bake 35 to 40 minutes, stirring vegetables after 20 minutes, until potatoes are tender and juice of chicken is no longer pink when centers of thickest pieces are cut.

1 Serving: Calories 420 (Calories from Fat 65); Fat 7g (Saturated 2g); Cholesterol 75mg; Sodium 780mg; Carbohydrate 61g (Dietary Fiber 5g); Protein 34g • **% Daily Value:** Vitamin A 44%; Vitamin C 74%; Calcium 6%; Iron 24% • **Diet Exchanges:** 4 Starch, 3 Very Lean Meat

chicken breasts with orange glaze

Your favorite preserve—such as apricot, peach or pineapple—can be used in place of the orange marmalade. This dish is especially delicious when served with rice. Try steamed green beans on the side.

prep 10 min • **cook** 20 min

1 1/2 teaspoons butter or margarine, melted

2 boneless, skinless chicken breast halves (about 1/2 pound)

1/2 teaspoon cornstarch

1/4 teaspoon ground mustard

1/4 cup orange juice

2 tablespoons orange marmalade

1 tablespoon soy sauce

1. Melt butter in 8-inch skillet or 3-quart saucepan over medium heat. Cook chicken in butter about 15 minutes, turning once, until juice of chicken is no longer pink when center of thickest piece is cut.

2. While chicken is cooking, mix cornstarch and mustard in small bowl. Stir in remaining ingredients.

3. Place chicken on serving plate; cover to keep warm. Discard any juices left in the skillet.

4. To make the glaze, pour orange mixture into skillet. Heat to boiling over medium heat, stirring constantly. Boil about 1 minute, stirring constantly, until glaze is thickened. Pour over chicken.

1 Serving: Calories 240 (Calories from Fat 65); Fat 7g (Saturated 3g); Cholesterol 80mg; Sodium 580mg; Carbohydrate 17g (Dietary Fiber 0g); Protein 27g • **% Daily Value:** Vitamin A 2%; Vitamin C 10%; Calcium 2%; Iron 6% • **Diet Exchanges:** 4 Very Lean Meat; 1 Fruit; 1 Fat

cantonese chicken chop suey

prep 10 min • **cook** 25 min

1/2 cup uncooked regular long-grain rice

2 boneless, skinless chicken breast halves (about 1/2 pound)

1/4 teaspoon peppered seasoned salt

1/2 bag (1-pound size) fresh (refrigerated) stir-fry vegetables (2 cups)

1/4 cup water

1/4 cup classic-style stir-fry sauce

1 1/2 teaspoons honey

1 cup chow mein noodles

2 tablespoons cashew pieces

1. Cook rice as directed on package.

2. While rice is cooking, cut chicken into 1/2-inch pieces. Spray 10-inch nonstick skillet with cooking spray; heat over medium-high heat. Add chicken; sprinkle with seasoned salt. Stir-fry 4 to 6 minutes or until brown.

3. Add vegetables and water to skillet. Heat to boiling; reduce heat to medium. Cover and cook 5 to 7 minutes, stirring occasionally, until vegetables are crisp-tender. Stir in stir-fry sauce and honey; heat through. Divide rice and noodles among bowls. Top with chicken mixture. Sprinkle with cashews.

1 Serving: Calories 545 (Calories from Fat 135); Fat 15g (Saturated 3g); Cholesterol 70mg; Sodium 1790mg; Carbohydrate 71g (Dietary Fiber 5g); Protein 37g • **% Daily Value:** Vitamin A 62%; Vitamin C 30%; Calcium 8%; Iron 28% • **Diet Exchanges:** 4 Starch; 3 Lean Meat, 2 Vegetable; 1 Fat

cantonese chicken chop suey

teriyaki chicken stir-fry

If you have the time, make quick-cooking brown rice to go with this flavorful stir-fry. Fruit salad sprinkled with toasted coconut makes a perfect dessert to follow.

prep 5 min • cook 15 min

2 boneless, skinless
chicken breast halves
(about 1/2 pound)

2 tablespoons vegetable oil

1 cup frozen crinkle-cut or
sliced carrots, thawed

1 cup frozen asparagus,
cut and thawed

3 tablespoons teriyaki sauce

3 tablespoons water

1. Cut chicken breast halves into bite-size pieces.

2. Heat wok or 10-inch skillet over high heat until 1 or 2 drips of water bubble and skitter when sprinkled in wok. Add 1 tablespoon oil; rotate wok to coat side. Add chicken; stir-fry about 4 minutes or until no longer pink in center. Remove chicken from wok.

3. Add remaining tablespoon oil to wok; rotate wok to coat side. Add carrots and asparagus; stir-fry 3 to 4 minutes or until vegetables are crisp-tender. Stir in teriyaki sauce and water. Cook and stir until bubbly. Stir in chicken. Cook and stir until heated through.

1 Serving: Calories 285 (Calories from Fat 115); Fat 13g (Saturated 2g); Cholesterol 70mg; Sodium 1150mg; Carbohydrate 16g (Dietary Fiber 4g); Protein 30g • **% Daily Value:** Vitamin A 100%; Vitamin C 18%; Calcium 6%; Iron 12% • **Diet Exchanges:** 3 1/2 Lean Meat, 3 Vegetable

chicken amandine

Toasting the almonds first gives the crispy coating for oven-baked chicken a more pronounced almond flavor. To toast the nuts, sprinkle them in an ungreased heavy skillet and cook over medium heat, stirring constantly, until golden brown, about 5 minutes.

prep 5 min • **bake** 25 min

3 tablespoons fine dry bread crumbs

3 tablespoons finely chopped toasted almonds

1 teaspoon chopped fresh or 1/4 teaspoon dried savory leaves

2 boneless, skinless chicken breast halves (about 1/2 pound)

2 tablespoons butter or margarine, melted

1. Heat oven to 375°. Grease square baking dish, 8 × 8 × 2 inches.

2. Mix bread crumbs, almonds and savory in shallow bowl. Dip chicken breast halves in butter, then coat with crumb mixture. Place in baking dish. Sprinkle with any remaining crumb mixture, and drizzle with any remaining butter.

3. Bake uncovered 20 to 25 minutes or until juices of chicken are no longer pink when center of thickest piece is cut.

1 Serving: Calories 240 (Calories from Fat 190); Fat 21g (Saturated 9g); Cholesterol 105mg; Sodium 230mg; Carbohydrate 9g (Dietary Fiber 1g); Protein 30g • **% Daily Value:** Vitamin A 8%; Vitamin C 0%; Calcium 6%; Iron 10% • **Diet Exchanges:** 1/2 Starch, 4 Lean Meat

asian tacos

good 2 know Flour tortillas make great Chinese pancakes and are a fun way to serve your favorite stir-fry dishes.

prep 10 min • **cook** 8 min

1 1/2 teaspoons vegetable oil

2 boneless, skinless chicken breast halves (about 1/2 pound), cut into thin strips

1/2 bag (1-pound size) frozen broccoli, red peppers, onions and mushrooms

1/4 cup stir-fry sauce

4 flour tortillas (8 inches in diameter)

Additional stir-fry sauce, if desired

1. Heat oil in 10-inch skillet or wok over high heat. Add chicken; stir-fry 3 to 4 minutes or until no longer pink in center. Remove from heat.

2. Cut vegetables into about 1/2-inch pieces; add to chicken in skillet. Stir-fry over medium-high heat about 2 minutes or until vegetables are crisp-tender; drain. Add stir-fry sauce. Cook and stir about 2 minutes or until hot.

3. Spread about 1/2 cup of the chicken mixture over half of each tortilla; fold tortillas in half. (Fold tortillas in half again if desired.) Serve with stir–fry sauce.

table for 2 For a stylish Asian dinner, set the table with chopsticks and brew a pot of jasmine tea. For dessert, set out a plate of pineapple chunks or fresh orange wedges. It's much more delicious than takeout!

1 Serving: Calories 495 (Calories from Fat 125); Fat 14g (Saturated 3g); Cholesterol 75mg; Sodium 1860mg; Carbohydrate 60g (Dietary Fiber 5g); Protein 38g • **% Daily Value:** Vitamin A 42%; Vitamin C 54%; Calcium 14%; Iron 28% • **Diet Exchanges:** 3 Starch; 3 1/2 Lean Meat; 3 Vegetable

asian tacos

cornish hen with bulgur

Cornish hen is the perfect size bird to roast whole for two. Add bulgur (a cracked whole wheat grain) for the hearty stuffing mixture and serve with sautéed carrots for an elegantly romantic meal.

prep 20 min • **stand** 15 min • **bake** 1 hr 15 min • *photograph on page 137*

Bulgur-Bacon Stuffing (below)

1 Rock Cornish hen (about 1 1/2 pounds)

1 tablespoon butter or margarine, melted

1. Prepare Bulgur-Bacon Stuffing. Heat oven to 350°.

2. Fill body cavity of hen with stuffing. Fasten opening with skewer. Place hen, breast side up, on rack in shallow roasting pan. Place meat thermometer in thigh muscle so tip does not touch bone. Brush hen with some of the butter.

3. Bake uncovered 1 to 1 1/4 hours, brushing occasionally with remaining butter, until thermometer reads 180° and juices are no longer pink when center of thigh is cut.

4. Remove stuffing from body cavity. Cut hen in half along backbone from tail to neck with kitchen scissors. Serve each hen half with stuffing.

bulgur-bacon stuffing

1 slice bacon, chopped

1 small onion, chopped (1/4 cup)

1/4 cup water

1 teaspoon chicken bouillon granules

3 tablespoons uncooked bulgur

1/4 cup shredded zucchini

1/4 cup chopped mushrooms

1 tablespoon dried cranberries or cherries, if desired

1/2 teaspoon chopped fresh or 1/8 teaspoon dried thyme leaves

Cook bacon and onion in 1-quart saucepan over medium-high heat, stirring frequently, until bacon is cooked and onion is tender. Drain bacon and onion. Heat water and bouillon granules to boiling in same saucepan. Stir in bulgur; remove from heat. Cover and let stand 15 minutes. Sir in bacon mixture, zucchini, mushrooms, cranberries and thyme.

tablefor 2

For Thanksgiving, if the two of you are planning to celebrate this favorite holiday together, Cornish hen is perfect in place of a big bird that will have you eating leftovers for weeks. Here are some delicious side dish and dessert suggestions to round out your holiday menu:

Buttercup Squash with Apples (page 130)
Asparagus Parmesan (page 132)
Orange-Pecan Muffins (page 156)
Fruit Trifle (page 182)

1 Serving: Calories 590 (Calories from Fat 360); Fat 40g (Saturated 13g); Cholesterol 255mg; Sodium 840mg; Carbohydrate 15g (Dietary Fiber 3g); Protein 45g • **% Daily Value:** Vitamin A 10%; Vitamin C 4%; Calcium 4%; Iron 12% • **Diet Exchanges:** 5 1/2 Medium-Fat Meat, 3 Vegetable

turkey and rice olé

good 2 know This dish tastes great and is even faster when made with leftover rice. Instead of cooking the instant rice, just add 1 cup cooked rice to the turkey in the skillet.

prep 5 min • **cook** 12 min

1/2 pound uncooked turkey breast slices or 2 boneless, skinless chicken breast halves (about 1/2 pound)

1/2 cup uncooked instant rice

1 tablespoon olive or vegetable oil

1/2 cup chunky salsa

1/2 cup shredded Cheddar cheese (2 ounces)

1. Cut turkey into bite-size pieces. Cook rice as directed on package.

2. Meanwhile, heat oil in 10-inch skillet over medium heat until hot. Cook turkey in oil about 4 minutes, stirring frequently, until no longer pink in center; drain.

3. Stir cooked rice and salsa into turkey in skillet; heat through. Sprinkle with cheese; reduce heat. Cover and cook 1 to 2 minutes or until cheese is melted.

1 Serving: Calories 415 (Calories from Fat 160); Fat 18g (Saturated 7g); Cholesterol 105mg; Sodium 510mg; Carbohydrate 28g (Dietary Fiber 1g); Protein 36g • **% Daily Value:** Vitamin A 14%; Vitamin C 6%; Calcium 18%; Iron 18% • **Diet Exchanges:** 2 Starch, 4 Lean Meat, 1 Fat

turkey with mushrooms and wine

 good 2 know   Serve this flavorful turkey and mushroom dish with wild rice or your favorite rice blend. In the fall, when lots of different varieties of mushrooms are available, use any mix of sliced mushrooms for the sauce.

prep 10 min • **cook** 15 min • *photograph on page 149*

1/2 pound uncooked turkey breast slices or turkey tenderloin, 1/4 to 1/2 inch thick

Salt

2 teaspoons butter or margarine

1 small clove garlic, finely chopped

1/3 cup dry red wine or beef broth

1 tablespoon tomato paste

3 cups sliced mushrooms (about 8 ounces)

1 green onion, chopped, if desired

1. If turkey pieces are more than 1/2 inch thick, flatten between plastic wrap or waxed paper. Sprinkle turkey breast slices lightly with salt.

2. Heat butter and garlic in 10-inch skillet over medium heat until hot. Cook turkey in butter 8 to 10 minutes, turning once, until no longer pink in center. Remove turkey from skillet; keep warm.

3. Mix wine and tomato paste in skillet. Stir in mushrooms. Cook uncovered 3 to 5 minutes, stirring occasionally, until mushrooms are tender. Serve mushroom mixture over turkey. Sprinkle with onion.

1 Serving: Calories 185 (Calories from Fat 45); Fat 5g (Saturated 3g); Cholesterol 85mg; Sodium 910mg; Carbohydrate 7g (Dietary Fiber 2g); Protein 30g • **% Daily Value:** Vitamin A 6%; Vitamin C 6%; Calcium 2%; Iron 12% • **Diet Exchanges:** 4 Very Lean Meat, 1 Vegetable, 1/2 Fat

vegetable-turkey loaf

good2know No need to make meat loaf for a crowd. It's also a perfect dish for two. If you don't have chili sauce on hand, try barbecue sauce or Russian dressing for a deliciously different topping.

prep 10 min • **bake** 45 min

1/2 pound ground turkey

1 slice bread, torn into small pieces

2 eggs or 1/4 cup fat-free cholesterol-free egg product or 2 egg whites

1/4 cup shredded carrot

2 tablespoons chopped onion

2 tablespoons chopped green bell pepper

2 tablespoons chopped celery

2 tablespoons chili sauce or ketchup

1/8 teaspoon salt

Dash of pepper

Dash of garlic powder

2 tablespoons chili sauce or ketchup

1. Heat oven to 350°.

2. Mix all ingredients except the last 2 tablespoons chili sauce. Shape mixture into loaf in center of ungreased shallow baking pan. Spoon 2 tablespoons chili sauce over loaf.

3. Bake uncovered about 45 minutes or until no longer pink in the center.

1 Serving: Calories 250 (Calories from Fat 65); Fat 7g (Saturated 2g); Cholesterol 75mg; Sodium 760mg; Carbohydrate 19g (Dietary Fiber 2g); Protein 30g • **% Daily Value:** Vitamin A 60%; Vitamin C 12%; Calcium 4%; Iron 10% • **Diet Exchanges:** 1/2 Starch, 3 1/2 Very Lean Meat, 2 Vegetable, 1 Fat

smothered orange roughy

Half the fun of cooking food in a packet is opening it at the table! Take the pouches to the table on plates and open for a tasty treat.

prep 5 min • **marinate** 15 min • **bake** 15 min

1/2 cup lemon juice

1 teaspoon walnut, avocado or vegetable oil

1/2 pound orange roughy or other mild-flavored fish fillets

1 1/2 teaspoons chopped fresh or 1/2 teaspoon dried marjoram leaves

1/8 teaspoon salt

2 medium roma (plum) tomatoes, chopped (3/4 cup)

1/2 bell pepper, cut into rings

1 small onion, sliced (3/4 cup)

1. Mix lemon juice and walnut oil. Pour over fillets. Cover and refrigerate at least 15 minutes but not more than 1 hour. Drain fish; discard marinade.

2. Heat oven to 375°.

3. Place fish fillets on 12- to 15-inch piece of aluminum foil or parchment paper and sprinkle with marjoram and salt. Top with tomatoes, bell pepper and onion. Wrap fish in foil, sealing tightly. Place on cookie sheet. Bake 15 minutes or until fish flakes easily with fork.

1 Serving: Calories 155 (Calories from Fat 20); Fat 2g (Saturated 0g); Cholesterol 60mg; Sodium 250mg; Carbohydrate 8g (Dietary Fiber 2g); Protein 23g • **% Daily Value:** Vitamin A 10%; Vitamin C 34%; Calcium 2%; Iron 4% • **Diet Exchanges:** 3 Very Lean Meat, 2 Vegetable

smothered orange roughy

hawaiian broiled cod with rice

good 2 know — Try an aromatic rice, like jasmine or basmati rice, to give this dinner tropical flair. Jasmine has a perfumy aroma while basmati is more nutty.

prep 7 min • **marinate** 5 min • **broil** 8 min

1 can (8 ounces) pineapple in juice, drained and juice reserved

2 tablespoons orange juice

1 teaspoon grated orange peel

2 teaspoons soy sauce

1/2 pound cod or other firm white fish fillet

2 cups hot cooked rice

1/2 orange, peeled and chopped

1 green onion, chopped

1 tablespoon coconut, toasted if desired

1. Set oven control to broil. Spray broiler pan with cooking spray.

2. Mix 1/3 cup of the reserved pineapple juice, the orange juice, orange peel and soy sauce. Cut fillet into 2 pieces. Marinate fish in sauce 5 minutes; remove.

3. Place fish on rack in broiler pan. Broil fish with tops 4 to 5 inches from heat 6 to 8 minutes or until fish flakes easily with fork.

4. Meanwhile, heat marinade to boiling in 1-quart saucepan; reduce heat to low. Simmer 3 minutes, stirring occasionally. Toss marinade with pineapple, rice, orange and green onion.

5. Serve fish over fruited rice. Top with toasted coconut, if desired.

table for 2 — The great escape! You're off to Hawaii when you serve this luscious fish and rice dish with steamed snow peas on the side. Place a single exotic flower bloom in a slim vase and turn on some island tunes for atmosphere.

1 Serving: Calories 385 (Calories from Fat 20); Fat 2g (Saturated 0g); Cholesterol 60mg; Sodium 320mg; Carbohydrate 68g (Dietary Fiber 3g); Protein 27g • **% Daily Value:** Vitamin A 4%; Vitamin C 26%; Calcium 6%; Iron 14% • **Diet Exchanges:** 2 Starch, 3 Very Lean Meat, 2 Fruit

easy fish and vegetable packets

good know

Foil packets are great for easy meals because the main dish, vegetables and sauce cook at the same time. Best of all, cleanup is a snap!

prep 5 min • **bake** 35 min

2 frozen sole, perch or other lean fish fillets (about 1/2 pound)

2 cups frozen mixed broccoli, cauliflower and carrots

1 1/2 teaspoons chopped fresh or 1/2 teaspoon dried dill weed

1/4 teaspoon salt

1/8 teaspoon pepper

2 tablespoons dry white wine or chicken broth

1. Heat oven to 450°.

2. Place each frozen fish fillet on 12-inch square of aluminum foil. Top each fillet with 1 cup of the vegetables. Sprinkle with dill weed, salt and pepper. Pour 1 tablespoon wine over each. Fold up sides of foil to make tent; fold top edges over to seal. Fold in sides, making a packet; fold to seal.

3. Place packets on cookie sheet. Bake about 35 minutes or until vegetables are crisp-tender and fish flakes easily with fork.

1 Serving: Calories 170 (Calories from Fat 20); Fat 2g (Saturated 1g); Cholesterol 90mg; Sodium 460mg; Carbohydrate 7g (Dietary Fiber 3g); Protein 24g • **% Daily Value:** Vitamin A 54%; Vitamin C 26%; Calcium 6%; Iron 6% • **Diet Exchanges:** 4 1/2 Very Lean Meat, 1 Vegetable

parsleyed parmesan fish

Mild-flavored fish varieties include cod, perch and catfish. Choose whatever is freshest in the fish section of your supermarket or purchase individually quick-frozen fillets so just one or two pieces (depending on the size) can be used at a time.

prep 3 min • **bake** 16 min

1/2 pound fresh or individually frozen (thawed) fish fillets

2 tablespoons grated Parmesan cheese

1 tablespoon Italian-style dry bread crumbs

1 tablespoon chopped fresh parsley

2 teaspoons butter or margarine, melted

1. Heat oven to 450°. Grease broiler pan rack.

2. Place fish fillets in single layer on rack in broiler pan. Mix remaining ingredients; sprinkle over fish. Bake uncovered 12 to 16 minutes or until fish flakes easily with fork.

1 Serving: Calories 170 (Calories from Fat 65); Fat 7g (Saturated 4g); Cholesterol 75mg; Sodium 260mg; Carbohydrate 3g (Dietary Fiber 0g); Protein 24g • **% Daily Value:** Vitamin A 8%; Vitamin C 2%; Calcium 10%; Iron 4% • **Diet Exchanges:** 3 1/2 Very Lean Meat, 1 Fat

parsleyed parmesan fish; hurry-up potato salad (page 141)

wine-poached salmon steak

good 2 know

What's the secret to perfectly moist fish prepared in minutes? Your microwave—it's perfect for poaching smaller quantities of fish like this salmon steak. Serve with steamed asparagus and a sourdough roll for a scrumptious meal!

prep 2 min • **microwave** 5 min

1 fresh or frozen (thawed) salmon steak (1/2 pound)

2 tablespoons dry white wine

2 tablespoons water

1/8 teaspoon salt

1/8 teaspoon pepper

1/8 teaspoon dried thyme

1/8 teaspoon dried tarragon

2 lemon slices (1/8 inch thick)

1. Place salmon steak in 14-ounce shallow casserole. Sprinkle with wine, water, salt, pepper, thyme and tarragon. Top with lemon slices.

2. Cover loosely with waxed paper and microwave on High (100%) until salmon flakes easily with fork, 3 to 5 minutes. Remove from casserole before serving.

1 Serving: Calories 140 (Calories from Fat 54); Fat 6g (Saturated 2g); Cholesterol 65mg; Sodium 210mg; Carbohydrate 1g (Dietary Fiber 0g); Protein 20g • **% Daily Value:** Vitamin A 2%; Vitamin C 0%; Calcium 0%; Iron 4% • **Diet Exchanges:** 3 Very Lean Meat, 1 Fat

caribbean swordfish

Try this juicy sweet salsa when summer peaches and nectarines are in season. Or try it with fresh mango for a delicious change.

prep 5 min • marinate 2 hours • broil 16 min

2 swordfish, shark or other medium-fat fish steaks, 1 inch thick (about 3/4 pound)

1 1/2 teaspoons grated lime peel

2 tablespoons lime juice

2 tablespoons grapefruit juice

1/4 teaspoon salt

1 small clove garlic, crushed

Peach Salsa (below)

1. Place fish steaks in a resealable plastic food-storage bag or shallow glass or plastic dish. Mix remaining ingredients, except salsa; pour over fish. Seal bag and refrigerate, turning fish once, at least 2 hours but no longer than 8 hours.

2. While fish is marinating, make Peach Salsa; cover and refrigerate.

3. Set oven control to broil. Spray broiler pan rack with cooking spray. Remove fish from marinade; reserve marinade. Place fish on rack in broiler pan. Broil with tops about 4 inches from heat about 16 minutes, turning and brushing once with marinade after 8 minutes, until fish flakes easily with fork. Discard any remaining marinade. Serve with salsa.

peach salsa

1 cup chopped fresh or frozen (thawed) peaches

2 tablespoons finely chopped red bell pepper

1 tablespoon finely chopped green onion

1 to 2 tablespoons grapefruit juice

2 teaspoons chopped fresh cilantro

Dash of salt

Mix all ingredients.

1 Serving: Calories 215 (Calories from Fat 65); Fat 7g (Saturated 2g); Cholesterol 80mg; Sodium 220mg; Carbohydrate 13g (Dietary Fiber 2g); Protein 27g • **% Daily Value:** Vitamin A 18%; Vitamin C 26%; Calcium 2%; Iron 6% • **Diet Exchanges:** 4 Very Lean Meat, 1 Fruit

scallops mornay

prep 25 min • **cook** 25 min

1/4 cup water or chicken broth

1 cup fresh or frozen asparagus, cut and thawed

2 tablespoons butter or margarine

1/2 pound bay or sea scallops

1 tablespoon all-purpose flour

1 teaspoon chopped fresh or 1/4 teaspoon dried chervil leaves

2/3 cup chicken broth

3/4 cup shredded Swiss cheese (3 ounces)

1 tablespoon dry sherry or chicken broth

2 cups hot cooked fettuccine or spinach fettuccine

1. Heat water to boiling in 1 1/2-quart saucepan. Add asparagus. Heat to boiling; reduce heat. Simmer uncovered about 4 minutes, stirring occasionally, until crisp-tender; drain.

2. Heat 1 tablespoon butter in same saucepan over medium-high heat until melted. Cook scallops in butter 3 to 5 minutes, stirring frequently, until scallops are white. Remove scallops from saucepan. Drain liquid.

3. Heat remaining 1 tablespoon butter in same saucepan until melted. Stir in flour and chervil. Cook over medium heat, stirring constantly, until smooth and bubbly; remove from heat. Stir in broth. Heat to boiling, stirring constantly. Boil and stir 1 minute.

4. Stir in cheese until melted. Stir in scallops, asparagus and sherry. Heat, stirring constantly, just until hot (do not boil). Serve scallop mixture over fettuccine.

1 Serving: Calories 575 (Calories from Fat 245); Fat 27g (Saturated 15g); Cholesterol 140mg; Sodium 690mg; Carbohydrate 50g (Dietary Fiber 3g); Protein 36g • **% Daily Value:** Vitamin A 30%; Vitamin C 12%; Calcium 52%; Iron 28% • **Diet Exchanges:** 3 Starch, 3 Lean Meat, 1 Vegetable, 3 Fat

garlic-almond shrimp

good2know Cook the rice together with the main course in this tasty casserole. To make this recipe even easier, purchase already peeled and deveined shrimp.

prep 20 min • **bake** 40 min • **stand** 3 min

1/2 pound fresh or frozen raw medium shrimp (in shells)

1 cup boiling water

1 cup sliced mushrooms (about 3 ounces)

1/2 cup uncooked regular long grain rice

1 small onion, thinly sliced

1 clove garlic, finely chopped

1/2 teaspoon salt

1/2 teaspoon ground ginger

1/2 cup whole almonds, toasted

1 can (11 ounces) mandarin orange segments, drained

1 package (6 ounces) frozen Chinese pea pods, thawed and drained

Soy sauce, if desired

1. Peel shrimp. (If shrimp are frozen, do not thaw; peel in cold water.) Make a shallow cut lengthwise down back of each shrimp; wash out vein.

2. Heat oven to 350°.

3. Mix water, mushrooms, rice, onion, garlic, salt, ginger and shrimp in ungreased square baking dish, 8 × 8 × 2 inches. Cover tightly with aluminum foil and bake 35 to 40 minutes or until liquid is absorbed and shrimp are pink.

4. Stir in remaining ingredients except soy sauce. Cover and let stand 3 minutes or until pea pods are hot. Serve with soy sauce.

1 Serving: Calories 535 (Calories from Fat 190); Fat 21g (Saturated 2g); Cholesterol 105mg; Sodium 720mg; Carbohydrate 71g (Dietary Fiber 10g); Protein 26g • **% Daily Value:** Vitamin A 20%; Vitamin C 70%; Calcium 16%; Iron 42% • **Diet Exchanges:** 4 Starch, 1 1/2 Lean Meat, 2 Vegetable, 2 Fat

mushroom-stuffed steak au poivre

Don't let the name fool you—this dish is simply a peppery broiled sirloin steak with a great mushroom stuffing!

prep 15 min • **cook** 22 min

1/2 pound beef boneless top sirloin steak, 1 1/2 inches thick

1/2 to 3/4 teaspoon freshly cracked pepper

1 tablespoon butter or margarine

3/4 cup sliced mushrooms (about 2 ounces)

2 medium green onions, sliced (2 tablespoons)

1 clove garlic, finely chopped

1. Cut outer edge of fat on beef steak diagonally at 1-inch intervals to prevent curling (do not cut into meat). Sprinkle both sides of beef with pepper; press pepper into beef. Cut a deep horizontal slit in beef to form a pocket.

2. Heat butter in 10-inch skillet over medium heat until melted. Cook mushrooms, onions and garlic in butter, stirring frequently, until mushrooms are tender; remove from heat.

3. Spoon mushroom mixture into pocket in beef. Close pocket opening by inserting 2 toothpicks in an X shape through edges of beef.

4. Set oven control to broil. Place beef on rack in broiler pan. Broil with tops 3 to 4 inches from heat about 6 minutes for rare or 8 minutes for medium. Turn beef; broil 5 minutes longer for rare or 7 minutes longer for medium. Remove toothpicks. Cut beef into halves.

1 Serving: Calories 230 (Calories from Fat 125); Fat 14g (Saturated 7g); Cholesterol 80mg; Sodium 100mg; Carbohydrate 2g (Dietary Fiber 1g); Protein 25g • **% Daily Value:** Vitamin A 8%; Vitamin C 2%; Calcium 2%; Iron 14% • **Diet Exchanges:** 3 1/2 Lean Meat, 1 Fat

pizza pot pies for two

good 2 know

Here's everything you love about pizza, baked in two small casseroles for a warming winter supper. For variety, add some of your favorite pizza toppings like chopped ripe olives or pepperoni slices (cut into fourths) to the pizza sauce mixture.

prep 15 min • bake 20 min

1/2 pound lean ground beef or Italian sausage

1/4 cup chopped onion

1/4 cup chopped green bell pepper

1/2 cup pizza sauce

1/2 cup sliced fresh mushrooms (about 2 ounces)

1/2 cup shredded mozzarella cheese

1/2 cup Original Bisquick

2 tablespoons very hot water

1. Heat oven to 375°. Grease two 10- to 12-ounce casseroles.

2. Cook ground beef, onion and bell pepper in 10-inch skillet over medium heat, stirring frequently, until beef is brown; drain. Stir in pizza sauce and mushrooms. Heat to boiling, stirring occasionally; reduce heat. Simmer uncovered 5 minutes, stirring occasionally. Spoon beef mixture into casseroles. Sprinkle 1/4 cup cheese on each.

3. Mix Bisquick and very hot water; beat vigorously 20 seconds. Turn dough onto surface dusted with Bisquick; gently roll in Bisquick to coat. Shape into ball; knead about 10 times or until smooth. Divide dough into 2 balls. Pat each ball into circle the size of diameter of casserole. Cut steam vent in each circle with knife or cookie cutter. Place each circle on beef mixture in casserole. Bake 15 to 20 minutes or until very light brown.

1 Serving: Calories 480 (Calories from Fat 235); Fat 28g (Saturated 11g); Cholesterol 80mg; Sodium 900mg; Carbohydrate 27g (Dietary Fiber 2g); Protein 32g • **% Daily Value:** Vitamin A 12%; Vitamin C 26%; Calcium 28%; Iron 20% • **Diet Exchanges:** 1 1/2 Starch; 4 Medium-Fat Meats; 1 Vegetable; 1 Fat

spicy beef stir-fry

good 2 know   If you're looking for a quick change from rice, try serving this stir-fry with soba noodles, a Japanese favorite. Made from buckwheat flour, they have a hearty nutty flavor.

prep 12 min • **cook** 12 min

2 teaspoons soy sauce

2 teaspoons cornstarch

1 to 2 teaspoons Chinese chili sauce with garlic

1 teaspoon and 1 tablespoon sesame or vegetable oil

1/2 pound beef flank steak, cut across grain into 1/8-inch strips

1 medium summer squash, cut into 1/4-inch slices (1 1/2 cups)

1/2 cup chicken broth

1/3 pound Chinese pea pods, cut diagonally into pieces (1 cup)

2 cups hot cooked rice or soba noodles

1. Mix soy sauce, cornstarch and chili sauce; reserve.

2. Heat wok or 10-inch nonstick skillet until 1 to 2 drops water bubble and skitter when sprinkled in wok. Add 1 teaspoon oil and rotate wok to coat bottom and side. Add beef. Stir-fry 2 to 3 minutes or until beef is brown; remove from wok.

3. Add remaining 1 tablespoon oil and rotate wok to coat side. Add squash. Stir-fry 1 minute. Add broth; cover and reduce heat to low. Cook 3 minutes or until squash is tender.

4. Stir in cornstarch mixture, pea pods and beef. Stir-fry over high heat 2 minutes or until pea pods are crisp-tender. Serve over rice.

1 Serving: Calories 445 (Calories from Fat 110); Fat 12g (Saturated 4g); Cholesterol 65mg; Sodium 660mg; Carbohydrate 55g (Dietary Fiber 4g); Protein 33g • **% Daily Value:** Vitamin A 10%; Vitamin C 38%; Calcium 8%; Iron 32% • **Diet Exchanges:** 3 Starch, 3 Lean Meat, 2 Vegetable

spicy beef stir-fry

pork chops with tomato relish

 good 2 know   These pork chops are topped with a tangy fresh tomato relish. The only side they need is warm cornbread or biscuits to mop up the delicious sauce.

prep 12 min • broil 11 min

1 small tomato, seeded and finely chopped (1/2 cup)

2 medium green onions, thinly sliced

1/4 cup finely chopped seeded cucumber

3 tablespoons Russian dressing

2 teaspoons white vinegar

3/4 teaspoon chopped fresh or 1/4 teaspoon dried tarragon leaves

1/2 teaspoon prepared mustard

2 pork loin or rib chops, 3/4 inch thick (about 3/4 pound)

1. Set oven control to broil.

2. Mix tomato, onions and cucumber in small bowl. Mix dressing, vinegar, tarragon and mustard in separate small bowl. Stir half of the dressing mixture into tomato mixture. Cover and refrigerate tomato relish. Reserve remaining dressing mixture.

3. Cut outer edge of fat on pork chops diagonally at 1-inch intervals to prevent curling (do not cut into meat). Place pork on rack in broiler pan.

4. Broil pork with tops about 4 inches from heat about 5 minutes or until brown. Turn pork; brush with dressing mixture. Broil 4 to 6 minutes longer for medium doneness (160°). Serve with tomato relish.

1 Serving: Calories 295 (Calories from Fat 155); Fat 17g (Saturated 4g); Cholesterol 75mg; Sodium 280mg; Carbohydrate 9g (Dietary Fiber 1g); Protein 27g • **% Daily Value:** Vitamin A 12%; Vitamin C 12%; Calcium 2%; Iron 8% • **Diet Exchanges:** 3 Lean Meat, 2 Vegetable, 1 1/2 Fat

peppercorn pork tenderloin

good 2 know Pork tenderloin is a tender, lower-fat and quick-to-fix meat. When you buy a whole tenderloin, cut it into 1/2-pound chunks to freeze for convenient two-person meals.

prep 5 min • **cook** 8 min

1 teaspoon olive oil

1/2 pound pork tenderloin, cut into 1/8-inch slices

1/2 teaspoon crushed green peppercorns

1/4 cup unsweetened apple juice

1 tablespoon lemon juice

1 tablespoon sour cream

Hot cooked orzo or rice, if desired

Chopped fresh parsley, if desired

1. Heat oil in 10-inch nonstick skillet over medium-high heat. Sprinkle both sides of pork with peppercorns.

2. Sauté pork in oil 1 to 2 minutes on each side or until brown. Stir apple juice and lemon juice into skillet. Cook over low heat 2 minutes or until pork is brown. Stir in sour cream until blended.

3. Serve pork and sauce over orzo. Sprinkle with parsley.

1 Serving: Calories 190 (Calories from Fat 70); Fat 8g (Saturated 3g); Cholesterol 75mg; Sodium 55mg; Carbohydrate 4g (Dietary Fiber 0g); Protein 26g • **% Daily Value:** Vitamin A 0%; Vitamin C 2%; Calcium 2%; Iron 8% • **Diet Exchanges:** 4 Very Lean Meat, 1 Fat

grilled creole pork and peppers

 Creole mustard, a spicy brown mustard, is a specialty of Louisiana. The same quantity of country-style Dijon mustard mixed with a dash of prepared horseradish can be substituted for Creole mustard.

prep 15 min • **grill** 15 min • **stand** 15 min

4 banana peppers or
2 Anaheim chilies

2 tablespoons tomato paste

2 tablespoons water

2 teaspoons red wine vinegar

1/2 teaspoon Worcestershire
sauce

1/2 teaspoon Creole mustard

1/2 teaspoon fresh or
1/8 teaspoon dried
thyme leaves

1 butterflied pork chop or
boneless loin chop, 3/4 inch
thick (1/2 pound)

1 teaspoon ground Cajun
seasoning blend for pork

1. Heat grill to low to moderate heat or set oven control to broil. Spray rack or broiler pan with cooking spray. Place peppers on grill or rack in broiler pan. Grill peppers 4 to 5 inches from heat about 4 minutes, turning several times, until skin is blistered and charred. Place peppers in paper bag. Close tightly; let stand 15 minutes.

2. Mix tomato paste, water, vinegar, Worcestershire sauce, mustard and thyme; set aside. Remove peppers from paper bag. Peel off skin; discard. Keep peppers warm.

3. Trim excess fat from pork chops. Slash outer edge of fat on pork 1/4-inch deep to prevent curling. Rub both sides of pork with Cajun seasoning blend. Place pork on rack or broiler pan.

4. Grill pork 4 to 5 inches from heat 4 minutes or until seasoning browns; brush with tomato sauce. Grill 1 minute; turn. Grill 3 minutes longer; brush with sauce. Grill 1 to 2 minutes longer. Heat remaining sauce to boiling; serve over pork and peppers.

1 Serving: Calories 215 (Calories from Fat 90); Fat 10g (Saturated 3g); Cholesterol 75mg; Sodium 210mg; Carbohydrate 13g (Dietary Fiber 2g); Protein 28g • **% Daily Value:** Vitamin A 16%; Vitamin C 100%; Calcium 2%; Iron 10% • **Diet Exchanges:** 3 Lean Meat, 3 Vegetable

grilled creole pork and peppers

italian kabobs

good 2 know — With green, white and red vegetables, here are all the colors of the Italian flag! For an elegant presentation, serve these festive kabobs on a bed of rice or couscous.

prep 10 min • **broil** 10 min • *photograph on page 2*

4 ten- or eleven-inch bamboo or metal skewers

1/2 pound fully cooked Polish sausage, cut into 1-inch pieces

1/2 small green bell pepper, cut into 1-inch pieces

8 medium whole mushrooms

1/4 cup creamy Italian or creamy garlic dressing

4 cherry tomatoes

1. If using bamboo skewers, soak in water at least 30 minutes before using to prevent burning. Set oven control to broil.

2. Thread sausage pieces, bell pepper pieces and mushrooms alternately on skewers, leaving space between each piece. Place kabobs on rack in broiler pan. Brush half of the dressing over kabobs.

3. Broil kabobs with tops about 4 inches from heat 5 minutes; turn. Add tomato to end of each skewer. Brush kabobs with remaining dressing. Broil about 5 minutes longer or until bell pepper pieces are crisp-tender.

1 Serving: Calories 455 (Calories from Fat 360); Fat 40g (Saturated 12g); Cholesterol 70mg; Sodium 1330mg; Carbohydrate 10g (Dietary Fiber 2g); Protein 16g • **% Daily Value:** Vitamin A 8%; Vitamin C 22%; Calcium 4%; Iron 12% • **Diet Exchanges:** 2 High-Fat Meat, 2 Vegetable, 4 1/2 Fat

lemon-tarragon lamb chops

good 2 know

Instead of roast leg of lamb for a spring celebration, try this quick and easy dish. Serve with oven-roasted new potatoes and steamed asparagus for a meal that highlights the freshest ingredients of the season!

prep 8 min • cook 22 min

2 lamb leg sirloin chops or 4 lamb rib chops, 1 inch thick (about 1 pound)

1/2 lemon

1 tablespoon olive or vegetable oil

1 cup sliced mushrooms (about 3 ounces)

1 medium green onion, thinly sliced

1 1/2 teaspoons chopped fresh or 1/2 teaspoon dried tarragon leaves

1 teaspoon lemon juice

1/2 teaspoon lemon pepper

3 tablespoons dry white wine or chicken broth

1/3 cup whipping (heavy) cream

1. Cut outer edge of fat on lamb chops diagonally at 1-inch intervals to prevent curling (do no cut into meat). Squeeze juice from 1/2 lemon over both sides of lamb.

2. Heat oil in 10-inch skillet over medium heat until hot. Cook lamb in oil 10 to 12 minutes for medium (160°), turning once. Remove lamb; keep warm. Drain fat from skillet, reserving 1 tablespoon in skillet.

3. Cook mushrooms, onion, tarragon, 1 teaspoon lemon juice and the lemon pepper in oil over medium-high heat 4 minutes, stirring occasionally. Stir in wine. Cook about 3 minutes, stirring occasionally, until liquid is reduced by half. Stir in whipping cream. Heat to boiling. Boil gently 1 minute. Serve mushroom mixture over lamb.

1 Serving: Calories 415 (Calories from Fat 250); Fat 28g (Saturated 12g); Cholesterol 155mg; Sodium 105mg; Carbohydrate 6g (Dietary Fiber 1g); Protein 36g • **% Daily Value:** Vitamin A 10%; Vitamin C 2%; Calcium 4%; Iron 18% • **Diet Exchanges:** 5 Medium-Fat Meat, 1 Vegetable

feta-stuffed lamb patties

good 2 know
These exotic-flavored "lamburgers" are just as delicious cooked on an outdoor grill. Put the buns on the grill to toast for a moment too.

prep 5 min • **broil** 14 min

1/2 pound ground lamb
or beef

2 tablespoons crumbled
feta cheese

2 tablespoons sour cream

1 tablespoon pesto

2 hamburger buns, split
and toasted

1. Set oven control to broil.

2. Shape ground lamb into 4 thin patties, about 4 inches in diameter. Place 1 tablespoon of the cheese on each of 2 patties. Top with remaining patties, pressing edges to seal in cheese. Place patties on rack in broiler pan.

3. Broil patties with tops about 4 inches from heat 6 to 7 minutes on each side until lamb is no longer pink in center.

4. Mix sour cream and pesto. Place patties on bottoms of buns. Top with pesto mixture and tops of buns.

table for 2

Make your breezy patio or terrace the setting for a Mediterranean feast when you serve these patties with Zucchini-Couscous Salad (page 20). A big bowl of fresh fruit or lemons makes a lovely, colorful centerpiece.

1 Serving: Calories 425 (Calories from Fat 245); Fat 27g (Saturated 11g); Cholesterol 90mg; Sodium 470mg; Carbohydrate 23g (Dietary Fiber 1g); Protein 24g • **% Daily Value:** Vitamin A 4%; Vitamin C 0%; Calcium 16%; Iron 18% • **Diet Exchanges:** 1 1/2 Starch, 3 Medium-Fat Meat, 2 Fat

feta-stuffed lamb patties; zucchini-couscous salad (page 20)

solutions for 2

perfect pasta

Pasta is a favorite quick dinner for two. For tasty sides, add a tossed green salad and some hearty bread or crunchy breadsticks. To cook pasta to *al dente* or "firm to the bite" perfection, follow these tips:

- **Use 2 ounces dried pasta** or 3 ounces refrigerated pasta for each serving. Fresh pasta cooks in about 1/4 the time of dried pasta, but cooking times will vary according to the shape.

- **Measure 4 ounces of spaghetti** (the perfect amount for two) easily by making a circle with your thumb and index finger the size of a quarter and filling it with pasta.

- **Choose a 3-quart saucepan** or larger for cooking pasta for two so the pasta can move freely in the boiling water during cooking.

- **Begin with cold water** and add 1 1/2 teaspoons salt for every 2 quarts of water. Bring the water to a full boil before adding pasta. It should remain boiling during the entire cooking time.

- **Find the best sauce** for the box of pasta that's already in your pantry, following this handy mix 'n' match guide:

Shape	Pasta	Sauce
Long thin or wide pastas	Capellini, Fettuccine, Linguine, Spaghetti, Vermicelli	Choose smooth, thin sauces or those with very finely chopped ingredients. They will cling better to the large surface area of these pasta shapes.
Short, wide and sturdy pastas	Mostaccioli, Penne, Rigatoni, Rotelle, Rotini, Ziti	Select chunky or heavy sauces. These pasta shapes are strong enough to hold up to larger pieces of ingredients.
Pastas with crevices and hollow areas	Cavatappi, Farfalle, Fusilli, Radiatore, Gemelli, Shells	Try sauces with small pieces of meat and vegetables that can be captured in the hollow areas of these pasta shapes.

chapter three

pasta pronto
and great grains

noodles, pasta casseroles and grains

black bean–pasta cancun

You'll enjoy this pasta with black beans and a south-of-the-border twist. It's also delicious with additions like chopped roast pork or grilled chicken tossed in.

prep 5 min • **cook** 12 min

2 cups uncooked radiatore pasta (4 ounces)

1 can (14 1/2 ounces) diced tomatoes with chili spices

1 cup black beans, rinsed and drained

1/2 teaspoon grated lime peel

1/4 teaspoon ground cumin

1/4 bell pepper, cut into 2 × 1/4-inch strips

2 tablespoons reduced-fat sour cream

2 lime wedges

Cilantro leaves, if desired

1. Cook pasta as directed on package. While pasta is cooking, heat tomatoes to boiling in 2-quart saucepan.

2. Drain pasta and stir into tomatoes with beans, lime peel, cumin and bell pepper; reduce heat to low. Cover and cook 2 to 3 minutes, stirring occasionally, until hot. Garnish with sour cream, lime and cilantro. Squeeze lime over pasta.

1 Serving: Calories 370 (Calories from Fat 35); Fat 4g (Saturated 1g); Cholesterol 5mg; Sodium 640mg; Carbohydrate 77g (Dietary Fiber 10g); Protein 17g • **% Daily Value:** Vitamin A 14%; Vitamin C 36%; Calcium 14%; Iron 30% • **Diet Exchanges:** 5 Starch

black bean–pasta cancun

fettuccine with ham and goat cheese

good 2 know

Serving long pastas, like fettuccine or linguine, can be tricky. A pair of kitchen tongs or a wooden pasta fork makes it a cinch! They allow you to easily grab the pasta and transfer it to your plate.

prep 10 min • **cook** 15 min

8 ounces uncooked fresh refrigerated or 4 ounces uncooked dried fettuccine or spinach fettuccine

3/4 cup diced fully cooked smoked ham

1/2 cup sour cream

1/2 cup milk

1 tablespoon butter or margarine

2 medium green onions, thinly sliced (2 tablespoons)

1/4 cup sliced pitted ripe olives

1/4 cup crumbled goat cheese (such as Montrachet) or feta cheese (1 ounce)

1 tablespoon chopped fresh parsley

Freshly ground pepper

1. Cook fettuccine as directed on package.

2. While fettuccine is cooking, heat ham, sour cream, milk, butter and onions in 1-quart saucepan over low heat, stirring constantly, just until hot. Stir in olives.

3. Drain fettuccine. Toss fettuccine with ham mixture. Sprinkle with cheese, parsley and pepper.

1 Serving: Calories 545 (Calories from Fat 280); Fat 31g (Saturated 16g); Cholesterol 155mg; Sodium 1210mg; Carbohydrate 45g (Dietary Fiber 3g); Protein 25g • **% Daily Value:** Vitamin A 24%; Vitamin C 4%; Calcium 26%; Iron 22% • **Diet Exchanges:** 3 Starch, 2 High-Fat Meat, 2 1/2 Fat

triple cheese ravioli

All the flavors of lasagna, but in a simple-to-prepare and quick-to-bake dish! For variety, try it with a different flavor of ravioli, like spinach or mushroom.

prep 25 min • **bake** 20 min

4 ounces dried cheese-filled ravioli or tortellini (about 1 cup)

1/2 cup sliced mushrooms (about 1 1/2 ounces)

2 tablespoons chopped onion

1 tablespoon chopped fresh or 1 teaspoon dried basil leaves

2 tablespoons dry red wine or chicken broth

Dash of salt

Dash of pepper

1 large tomato, chopped (1 cup)

1 clove garlic, finely chopped

1/2 cup ricotta cheese

2 tablespoons grated Parmesan cheese

1. Heat oven to 325°. Cook ravioli as directed on package.

2. While ravioli is cooking, cook remaining ingredients except cheeses in 10-inch skillet over medium-high heat about 5 minutes, stirring frequently, until tomato is soft.

3. Drain ravioli. Place ravioli in ungreased loaf dish, 9 × 5 × 3 inches. Spread ricotta cheese over ravioli. Pour tomato sauce over top. Sprinkle with Parmesan cheese. Bake uncovered about 20 minutes or until hot.

1 Serving: Calories 250 (Calories from Fat 110); Fat 12g (Saturated 6g); Cholesterol 80mg; Sodium 670mg; Carbohydrate 20g (Dietary Fiber 2g); Protein 17g • **% Daily Value:** Vitamin A 26%; Vitamin C 14%; Calcium 36%; Iron 10% • **Diet Exchanges:** 1 Starch, 1 1/2 High-Fat Meat, 1 Vegetable

dilled fettuccine with whiskey-crab sauce

good 2 know Short on time? Speed up preparation time by using refrigerated fettuccine. It cooks much faster than the dried variety.

prep 8 min • **cook** 12 min

4 ounces uncooked fettuccine

1 jar (6 ounces) marinated artichoke hearts, drained

1 tablespoon butter or margarine

3 medium green onions, sliced

1/2 cup Scotch whiskey, bourbon or chicken broth

1 1/2 teaspoons chopped fresh or 1/2 teaspoon dried dill weed

1/8 teaspoon salt

1/8 teaspoon pepper

3/4 cup whipping (heavy) cream

1 cup cut-up cooked crabmeat, or frozen (thawed) salad-style imitation crabmeat or 1 can (6 ounces) crabmeat, drained and cartilage removed

1/4 cup slivered almonds, toasted

1. Cook fettuccine as directed on package.

2. Cut artichoke hearts into halves if necessary. Heat butter in 10-inch skillet over medium heat until melted. Cook 2 tablespoons green onions in butter about 3 minutes, stirring frequently, until tender. Stir in whiskey, dill weed, salt and pepper. Cook over medium-high heat about 3 minutes, stirring occasionally, until almost all liquid has evaporated.

3. Stir whipping cream into whiskey mixture. Heat to boiling, stirring constantly. Cook over medium-high heat about 3 minutes, stirring frequently, until slightly thickened. Stir in artichoke hearts and crabmeat; heat through.

4. Drain fettuccine. Toss fettuccine and sauce. Sprinkle with slivered almonds and remaining green onions.

1 Serving: Calories 710 (Calories from Fat 415); Fat 46g (Saturated 23g); Cholesterol 230mg; Sodium 690mg; Carbohydrate 53g (Dietary Fiber 8g); Protein 29g • **% Daily Value:** Vitamin A 32%; Vitamin C 12%; Calcium 24%; Iron 26% • **Diet Exchanges:** 3 Starch, 2 High-Fat Meat, 2 Vegetable, 4 Fat

dilled fettuccine with whiskey-crab sauce

easy chicken-pasta primavera

 good 2 know   If you like ranch dressing in salad, you'll love how it becomes a delicious and super easy creamy sauce for pasta.

prep 10 min • **cook** 10 min

4 ounces uncooked fettuccine

1 cup broccoli flowerets

1/2 cup 1/4-inch strips carrot

1 teaspoon olive or vegetable oil

2 boneless, skinless chicken breast halves (about 1/2 pound), cut into 1/2-inch strips

1 clove garlic, finely chopped

1/3 cup ranch dressing

2 tablespoons grated Parmesan cheese

1 teaspoon shredded fresh or 1/8 teaspoon dried basil leaves

1. Cook fettuccine as directed on package adding broccoli and carrot 1 minute before pasta is done.

2. While fettuccine is cooking, heat oil in 10-inch nonstick skillet over medium-high heat until hot. Sauté chicken and garlic in oil 2 to 3 minutes until chicken is no longer pink in center; remove from heat. Stir in dressing, cheese and basil.

3. Drain fettuccine and vegetables. Toss fettuccine and vegetables with chicken mixture.

1 Serving: Calories 580 (Calories from Fat 260); Fat 29g (Saturated 5g); Cholesterol 140mg; Sodium 610mg; Carbohydrate 45g (Dietary Fiber 4g); Protein 39g • **% Daily Value:** Vitamin A 100%; Vitamin C 36%; Calcium 20%; Iron 22% • **Diet Exchanges:** 2 Starch, 4 Lean Meat, 3 Vegetable, 3 Fat

sichuan eggplant linguine

good 2 know

Use any thin-strand pasta, such as angel hair, Chinese noodles or even soba (buckwheat) noodles for this truly international dish. Sichuan (Szechuan) usually means fiery hot, so taste the sauce and adjust the heat level until it's right for you.

prep 8 min • **cook** 12 min

4 ounces uncooked linguine

1 teaspoon vegetable oil

1 medium Japanese eggplant, chopped (about 1 1/2 cups)

3/4 cup chunky garlic and onion spaghetti sauce

1 to 2 teaspoons Sichuan (Szechuan) hot and spicy sauce or Chinese chili sauce

1/2 teaspoon freshly grated gingerroot, if desired

1. Cook linguine as directed on package.

2. While linguine is cooking, heat oil in 1-quart saucepan over medium-high heat. Sauté eggplant in oil. Stir in spaghetti and Sichuan (Szechuan) sauces; reduce heat to medium. Cook 2 minutes, stirring occasionally, until hot.

3. Drain linguine and toss with eggplant sauce. Sprinkle with gingerroot.

1 Serving: Calories 385 (Calories from Fat 65); Fat 7g (Saturated 1g); Cholesterol 0mg; Sodium 510mg; Carbohydrate 80g (Dietary Fiber 10g); Protein 11g • **% Daily Value:** Vitamin A 18%; Vitamin C 14%; Calcium 4%; Iron 20% • **Diet Exchanges:** 4 Starch, 1 Fruit

mushroom olive penne

Here's an easy weeknight dinner idea: add zip to your favorite spaghetti or marinara sauce with mushrooms, olives and paprika and serve over pasta. Try spinach salad with balsamic vinaigrette on the side.

prep 5 min • **cook** 15 min

1 1/2 cups uncooked penne pasta (4 ounces)

1 teaspoon olive oil

1 cup thinly sliced mushrooms (about 3 ounces)

1 medium onion, chopped (1/2 cup)

1 cup Italian-seasoned chunky tomato sauce

1 teaspoon paprika

12 pimento-stuffed olives

2 to 4 teaspoons grated Parmesan cheese

Basil leaves, if desired

1. Cook penne as directed on package.

2. While penne is cooking, heat oil in 2-quart saucepan over medium-high heat. Sauté mushrooms and onion in oil; reduce heat to medium. Stir in tomato sauce, paprika and olives.

3. Drain penne and add to tomato sauce. Cook stirring occasionally, until heated through. Sprinkle with cheese. Garnish with basil.

1 Serving: Calories 570 (Calories from Fat 10); Fat 12g (Saturated 2g); Cholesterol 0mg; Sodium 1240mg; Carbohydrate 106g (Dietary Fiber 7g); Protein 17g • **% Daily Value:** Vitamin A 18%; Vitamin C 18%; Calcium 10%; Iron 30% • **Diet Exchanges:** 6 Starch, 3 Vegetable, 1/2 Fat

hearty bean and pasta stew

Most of the ingredients for this hearty stew can be found right in your pantry. Feel free to use what you have on hand: any small pasta shape can be substituted for the macaroni; and the beans you like best—like navy, cannellini or butter beans—can replace the garbanzos and kidney beans.

prep 10 min • **cook** 15 min

1/2 cup uncooked shell macaroni

2 tablespoons chopped green bell pepper

2 tablespoons chopped onion

1 1/2 teaspoons chopped fresh or 1/2 teaspoon dried basil leaves

1/2 teaspoon Worcestershire sauce

1 small tomato, coarsely chopped (1/2 cup)

1 clove garlic, finely chopped

1/2 can (16 ounces) garbanzo beans, rinsed and drained (about 1 cup)

1 can (8 ounces) kidney beans, rinsed and drained

1 cup chicken broth

1. Mix all ingredients in 2-quart saucepan. Heat to boiling, stirring occasionally; reduce heat.

2. Cover and simmer about 15 minutes, stirring occasionally, until macaroni is tender.

1 Serving: Calories 430 (Calories from Fat 45); Fat 5g (Saturated 1g); Cholesterol 0mg; Sodium 840mg; Carbohydrate 86g (Dietary Fiber 15g); Protein 28g • **% Daily Value:** Vitamin A 8%; Vitamin C 16%; Calcium 10%; Iron 46% • **Diet Exchanges:** 5 Starch, 1 Vegetable

shrimp-pasta salad toss

What's the fastest way to toss a picnic salad together? Start with pasta salad from the deli and turn it into homemade by adding fresh vegetables and cooked shrimp.

prep 10 min

6 ounces frozen cooked shrimp, thawed

2 cups bite-size pieces spinach

1/2 pint deli pasta salad

1/2 cup cherry tomatoes, cut into halves

2 tablespoons sliced pitted ripe olives

1 to 2 tablespoons milk, if desired

1. Toss all ingredients except milk.

2. Add milk, a tablespoon at a time, if needed to thin the pasta salad dressing.

table for 2
Pack a small cooler and bring dinner to the park tonight! Keep it cool with Cold Gazpacho Soup (page 12) or chilled tomato juice. And don't forget your favorite cookies for dessert.

1 Serving: Calories 275 (Calories from Fat 90); Fat 10g (Saturated 2g); Cholesterol 175mg; Sodium 620mg; Carbohydrate 26g (Dietary Fiber 3g); Protein 23g • **% Daily Value:** Vitamin A 72%; Vitamin C 16%; Calcium 8%; Iron 28% • **Diet Exchanges:** 1 Starch, 2 Medium-Fat Meat, 2 Vegetable

shrimp-pasta salad toss; sesame fingers (page 159)

mushroom manicotti

prep 20 min • bake 20 min

4 uncooked manicotti shells

Garlic-Mushroom Sauce (below)

1 package (3 ounces) cream cheese, softened

3 tablespoons crumbled feta cheese

2 tablespoons chopped onion

1/2 teaspoon Worcestershire sauce

1/4 cup diced fully cooked smoked ham

1 tablespoon chopped fresh or 1 teaspoon freeze-dried chives

1. Heat oven to 350°. Cook manicotti shells as directed on package; drain. Prepare Garlic-Mushroom Sauce in same saucepan.

2. Mix cream cheese, feta cheese, onion and Worcestershire sauce in small bowl, using fork, until well blended. Stir in ham and chives. Fill each shell with about 3 tablespoons of the cheese mixture, using small spoon.

3. Pour half of the sauce into ungreased square baking dish, 8 × 8 × 2 inches. Arrange filled shells in baking dish. Spoon remaining sauce over shells. Cover with aluminum foil and bake about 20 minutes or until hot and bubbly.

garlic-mushroom sauce

1 tablespoon butter or margarine

2 cups sliced mushrooms (about 5 ounces)

2 tablespoons chopped onion

2 cloves garlic, finely chopped

1/3 cup dry sherry, dry white wine or chicken broth

1 teaspoon lemon juice

1/4 teaspoon lemon pepper

1/8 teaspoon salt

1/2 cup whipping (heavy) cream

Heat butter in 3-quart saucepan over medium heat until melted. Cook mushrooms, onion and garlic in butter about 3 minutes, stirring frequently, until vegetables are crisp-tender. Stir in sherry, lemon juice, lemon pepper and salt. Cook over medium-high heat about 4 minutes, stirring occasionally, until almost all liquid has evaporated. Stir in whipping cream. Heat to boiling, stirring constantly. Boil over medium-high heat about 1 minute, stirring frequently, until slightly thickened.

1 Serving: Calories 625 (Calories from Fat 405); Fat 45g (Saturated 27g); Cholesterol 150mg; Sodium 780mg; Carbohydrate 40g (Dietary Fiber 3g); Protein 17g • **% Daily Value:** Vitamin A 32%; Vitamin C 6%; Calcium 16%; Iron 18% • **Diet Exchanges:** 2 1/2 Starch, 1 1/2 High-Fat Meat, 6 Fat

spinach-stuffed pinwheels

good 2 know Lasagna noodles are available with ruffled or straight edges. If you use the ruffled-edge ones, your pinwheels will look like pretty flowers!

prep 25 min • **bake** 20 min

2 uncooked lasagna noodles

1 package (10 ounces) frozen chopped spinach

1/2 cup small curd creamed cottage cheese

1 tablespoon chopped fresh or 1 teaspoon dried oregano leaves

1/4 teaspoon garlic powder

1 tablespoon butter or margarine

1 tablespoon all-purpose flour

1/4 teaspoon salt

1/8 teaspoon ground nutmeg

1 cup milk

1/2 cup shredded Swiss cheese (2 ounces)

1/2 cup shredded mozzarella cheese (2 ounces)

Grated Parmesan cheese, if desired

1. Cook noodles as directed on package; drain. Rinse in cold water; drain. Cut noodles lengthwise into halves.

2. While noodles are cooking, cook spinach as directed on package; drain thoroughly. Press spinach between several layers of paper towels to squeeze out excess liquid. Mix spinach, cottage cheese, oregano and garlic powder.

3. Heat oven to 350°. Grease 2 individual gratin dishes or oval 16-ounce casseroles.

4. Heat butter in 1 1/2-quart saucepan over medium heat until melted. Stir in flour, salt and nutmeg. Cook over medium heat, stirring constantly, until mixture is smooth and bubbly; remove from heat. Stir in milk. Heat to boiling, stirring constantly. Boil and stir 1 minute; reduce heat. Stir in Swiss and mozzarella cheeses until melted.

5. *Loosely* roll up each noodle strip. Arrange 2 noodle rolls, cut side down, in each dish. Spread each noodle roll gently apart, using fingers, until 2 1/2 inches in diameter, making space in center for spinach filling. Spoon spinach filling into noodle rolls. Pour cheese sauce over noodle rolls. Sprinkle with Parmesan cheese. Cover with aluminum foil and bake about 20 minutes or until hot and bubbly.

1 Serving: Calories 450 (Calories from Fat 205); Fat 23g (Saturated 15g); Cholesterol 70mg; Sodium 910mg; Carbohydrate 33g (Dietary Fiber 4g); Protein 32g • **% Daily Value:** Vitamin A 100%; Vitamin C 10%; Calcium 78%; Iron 14% • **Diet Exchanges:** 2 Starch, 3 Medium-Fat Meat, 1 Vegetable, 1 Fat

creamy zucchini lasagna

There's no better accompaniment to this creamy lasagna than crusty golden slices of garlic bread.

prep 25 min • **bake** 30 min • **stand** 10 min

2 uncooked lasagna noodles

1 tablespoon butter or margarine

1 medium zucchini, cut into julienne strips

2 tablespoons sliced green onions

2 cloves garlic, finely chopped

1 egg, beaten

1/2 cup ricotta or small curd creamed cottage cheese, drained

4 tablespoons grated Parmesan cheese

1 tablespoon chopped fresh or 1 teaspoon dried marjoram leaves

1 cup spaghetti sauce

1 cup shredded mozzarella cheese (4 ounces)

1. Heat oven to 350°. Cook noodles as directed on package; drain. Rinse in cold water; drain. Cut noodles crosswise into halves.

2. Heat butter in 10-inch skillet over medium heat until melted. Cook zucchini, onions and garlic in butter about 3 minutes, stirring frequently, until zucchini is crisp-tender; drain. Mix egg, ricotta cheese, 2 tablespoons of the Parmesan cheese and the marjoram.

3. Spread 1/4 cup of the spaghetti sauce in each of 2 ungreased individual 16-ounce casseroles or au gratin dishes. Top each with 1 noodle half. Spread one-fourth of the ricotta mixture over each noodle half. Top each with one-fourth of the zucchini mixture. Sprinkle each with one-fourth of the mozzarella cheese. Continue layering with remaining noodles, ricotta mixture, spaghetti sauce and zucchini mixture. Sprinkle with remaining mozzarella cheese and remaining 2 tablespoons Parmesan cheese.

4. Cover with aluminum foil and bake 20 minutes. Uncover and bake about 10 minutes longer or until hot and bubbly. Let stand 10 minutes before serving.

1 Serving: Calories 560 (Calories from Fat 290); Fat 38g (Saturated 17g); Cholesterol 180mg; Sodium 1300mg; Carbohydrate 48g (Dietary Fiber 4g); Protein 36g • **% Daily Value:** Vitamin A 52%; Vitamin C 24%; Calcium 82%; Iron 16% • **Diet Exchanges:** 3 Starch, 3 Medium-Fat Meat, 1 Vegetable, 2 Fat

cajun beef and rice

good **2** know Okra does double duty in this hearty main dish; it adds wonderful flavor and texture, and also thickens the sauce.

prep 10 min • **cook** 10 min

1/4 pound extra-lean ground beef

1 small stalk celery, chopped (1/4 cup)

1 small onion, chopped (1/4 cup)

1 teaspoon Cajun seasonings blend

1 cup uncooked instant rice

1/4 cup chopped green bell pepper

1/2 cup water

4 medium fresh or 1/2 cup frozen (thawed) okra, sliced

1 medium tomato, chopped (1/2 cup)

1 can (11 1/2 ounces) lightly tangy eight-vegetable juice

1. Heat 10-inch nonstick skillet over medium-high heat. Cook ground beef, celery, onion and Cajun seasoning blend, stirring frequently, 4 minutes or until beef is brown and vegetables are tender.

2. Stir in remaining ingredients. Reduce heat to medium-low. Cover and cook 5 minutes or until rice is tender.

1 Serving: Calories 380 (Calories from Fat 65); Fat 7g (Saturated 3g); Cholesterol 35mg; Sodium 590mg; Carbohydrate 65g (Dietary Fiber 5g); Protein 19g • **% Daily Value:** Vitamin A 48%; Vitamin C 70%; Calcium 8%; Iron 26% • **Diet Exchanges:** 4 Starch, 1 Very Lean Meat, 1 Vegetable

red beans and rice

This colorful main dish is sure to warm the soul. Serve it with hot-from-the-oven corn muffins—and offer a pot of honey butter for slathering on the muffins.

prep 12 min • **cook** 8 min

1 teaspoon vegetable oil

1 small onion, chopped (1/4 cup)

1 small green bell pepper, chopped (1/2 cup)

1 clove garlic, crushed

1 teaspoon chopped fresh or 1/4 teaspoon dried thyme leaves

1/4 teaspoon salt

1/2 teaspoon red pepper sauce

1 can (15 to 16 ounces) kidney beans, rinsed and drained

1/2 package (10 ounces) frozen cut okra, thawed

2 cups hot cooked rice

1 small tomato, seeded and chopped (about 1/4 cup)

1. Heat oil in 10-inch skillet over medium-high heat. Cook onion, bell pepper and garlic in oil about 2 minutes, stirring occasionally.

2. Stir in remaining ingredients except rice and tomato. Cook, stirring occasionally, until mixture is hot. Serve with rice. Top with tomato.

1 Serving: Calories 520 (Calories from Fat 35); Fat 4g (Saturated 1g); Cholesterol 0mg; Sodium 840mg; Carbohydrate 108g (Dietary Fiber 19g); Protein 26g • **% Daily Value:** Vitamin A 18%; Vitamin C 52%; Calcium 20%; Iron 52% • **Diet Exchanges:** 7 Starch, 1 Vegetable

red beans and rice

cheesy polenta

good 2 know Polenta is an Italian version of cornmeal mush. It's frequently mixed with cheese, molded and then baked, fried or grilled. It's often served topped with the sauce of your choice: meat, tomato, mushroom or cheese sauce all make delicious toppings.

cook 15 min • **chill** 1 hr • **bake** 50 min

1/2 cup cornmeal

1/2 cup cold water

1 1/2 cups boiling water

1/8 teaspoon salt

3/4 cup shredded sharp Cheddar cheese (3 ounces)

1 tablespoon chopped fresh or 1 teaspoon freeze-dried chives

1/4 cup grated Parmesan cheese

1/2 cup spaghetti sauce with meat

1. Grease two 10-ounce custard cups. Mix cornmeal and cold water in 1 1/2-quart saucepan. Stir in boiling water and salt. Cook over medium heat, stirring constantly, until mixture thickens and boils; reduce heat to low. Cover and simmer 10 minutes, stirring occasionally; remove from heat. Stir in Cheddar cheese and chives until cheese is melted.

2. Spread one-fourth of the cornmeal mixture in each custard cup. Sprinkle each with 1 tablespoon of the Parmesan cheese. Repeat with remaining cornmeal mixture and Parmesan cheese. Cover and refrigerate at least 1 hour until firm and chilled through.

3. Heat oven to 350°. Cover the custard cups with aluminum foil and bake about 50 minutes or until hot in center. Meanwhile, heat spaghetti sauce in 1-quart saucepan until bubbly. Unmold polenta. Serve with spaghetti sauce.

1 Serving: Calories 375 (Calories from Fat 180); Fat 20g (Saturated 12g); Cholesterol 55mg; Sodium 1060mg; Carbohydrate 32g (Dietary Fiber 3g); Protein 20g • **% Daily Value:** Vitamin A 18%; Vitamin C 6%; Calcium 40%; Iron 12% • **Diet Exchanges:** 2 Starch, 2 High-Fat Meat, 1 Vegetable

jambalaya

good 2 know

You might expect this recipe to make a huge pot of classic Cajun jambalaya, a favorite Louisiana rice dish. In fact, it's the perfect quantity for a hearty meal for two—the only extra you'll need is a bottle of hot sauce for adding at the table!

prep 15 min • **cook** 35 min

4 pork sausage links, cut into bite-size pieces

1/2 cup uncooked regular long grain rice

1/4 cup sliced celery

1/4 cup chopped green bell pepper

1 small onion, chopped (about 1/4 cup)

2 cloves garlic, finely chopped

1 can (8 ounces) stewed tomatoes

1 can (8 ounces) tomato sauce

1/2 cup water

1 1/2 teaspoons chopped fresh or 1/2 teaspoon dried thyme leaves

1/8 to 1/4 teaspoon ground red pepper (cayenne)

1/8 teaspoon salt

1 bay leaf

1/2 cup diced fully cooked smoked ham

Chopped fresh parsley, if desired

1. Cook sausage in 1 1/2-quart saucepan over medium heat, stirring frequently, until brown. Remove sausage and reserve. Drain fat from saucepan, reserving 2 tablespoons in saucepan.

2. Cook rice, celery, bell pepper, onion and garlic in fat in saucepan over medium-high heat about 6 minutes, stirring frequently, until rice is light brown.

3. Stir in tomatoes, tomato sauce, water, thyme, red pepper, salt and bay leaf. Heat to boiling; reduce heat to low. Cover and simmer about 20 minutes, stirring frequently, just until rice is tender. Stir in sausage and ham. Cover and simmer just until ham is hot. Remove bay leaf. Sprinkle with parsley.

1 Serving: Calories 420 (Calories from Fat 110); Fat 12g (Saturated 4g); Cholesterol 40mg; Sodium 2060mg; Carbohydrate 62g (Dietary Fiber 4g); Protein 20g • **% Daily Value:** Vitamin A 24%; Vitamin C 0%; Calcium 8%; Iron 22% • **Diet Exchanges:** 3 Starch, 1 Lean Meat, 3 Vegetable, 1 Fat

spinach-barley risotto

good 2 know Pearl barley gives this main dish the creaminess of traditional risotto made with Arborio rice. You can also use quick-cooking barley—it doesn't require presoaking, but the dish won't be as creamy.

soak 5 hours • **prep** 10 min • **cook** 23 min

3/4 cup pearl barley or uncooked quick-cooking barley

2 teaspoons olive oil

1 cup thinly sliced mushrooms (4 ounces)

1 medium onion, chopped (1/2 cup)

1 1/2 cups chicken or vegetable broth

1 teaspoon garlic pepper seasoning blend

1 teaspoon Dijon mustard

1/3 cup instant wild rice

1/4 cup dried cranberries

2 cups packed spinach leaves, shredded (3 ounces)

1. If using pearl barley, presoak in 2 cups of water at least 5 hours or overnight; drain.

2. Heat oil in 10-inch nonstick skillet over high heat. Cook mushrooms and onion in oil. Stir in broth, garlic pepper seasoning blend and mustard. Cover and heat to boiling.

3. Stir in remaining ingredients, except spinach; reduce heat to low. Cover and simmer 10 minutes, stirring once. Stir in spinach; cover and simmer about 5 minutes or until water is absorbed and barley and wild rice are tender.

1 Serving: Calories 465 (Calories from Fat 55); Fat 7g (Saturated 1g); Cholesterol 0mg; Sodium 870mg; Carbohydrate 102g (Dietary Fiber 17g); Protein 18g • **% Daily Value:** Vitamin A 56%; Vitamin C 12%; Calcium 8%; Iron 24% • **Diet Exchanges:** 6 Starch, 2 Vegetable

spinach-barley risotto

solutions for

2

table tailored for two

Creating a festive meal for two—whether breakfast, lunch or dinner—can be much more fun than cooking for four, six or larger numbers of people. Since it's just the two of you, you can enjoy the freedom of setting the table the way you want and eating the foods that *you* like.

- **Splurging for just two new settings** of dinnerware and flatware is easier and less expensive than buying a whole new set. Then, snap up some interesting place mats and napkins for two at great prices during "white sales" and seasonal closeouts to give your table new pizzazz.

- **Having the right-sized cooking equipment** makes it easier to prepare and serve meals for two. Stock your kitchen cabinets with smaller baking dishes, small loaf pans, individual pie or tart pans and six-cup muffin pans. Look for attractive individual casseroles, au gratin dishes and custard cups that can go directly from the oven to the table.

- **Planning lively meals** with foods that have a variety of flavors, textures, colors, shapes or temperatures makes mealtime more fun and interesting. Follow your mood depending on the season, the weather or if you have a fun occasion to celebrate.

- **Choosing the main course first**—whether it's meat or meatless—makes it easier to plan the rest of the meal. Some days you'll want a vegetable and potatoes or rice on the side; on other days, a tossed green salad or some good bread are enough.

- **There's no rule** that says you must have a main course plus sides for dinner every day. You may prefer to have your heaviest meal at noon with a light supper in the evening. Some days a soup or salad fits the bill; on busy days a sandwich may be the answer. Eggs and pancakes also make great dinners!

- **For a change of pace,** try a picnic—indoors or out! Serve dinner in the family room, at the coffee table, on the porch or in the backyard. Or get really adventurous and pack up a basket for the park, the beach or an outdoor concert.

chapter four

brunch
with ease

breakfast all day long

mediterranean eggs

> **good 2 know** This is a delicious brunch dish for summer, when tomatoes are at their ripest and fresh basil is most fragrant.

prep 5 min • **cook** 10 min

1 teaspoon vegetable oil

3 green onions, chopped (1/4 cup)

1 medium tomato, chopped (1/2 cup)

1 tablespoon chopped fresh or 1 teaspoon dried basil leaves

1 cup fat-free cholesterol-free egg product or 4 eggs

Freshly ground pepper

1. Heat oil in 8-inch nonstick skillet over medium heat. Cook onions in oil 2 minutes; stir in tomato and basil. Cook, stirring occasionally, about 1 minute or until tomato is heated through. Pour egg product over tomato mixture.

2. As mixture begins to set at bottom and side, gently lift cooked portions with spatula so that thin, uncooked portion can flow to bottom. Avoid constant stirring. Cook 3 to 4 minutes or until eggs are thickened throughout but still moist. Sprinkle with pepper.

1 Serving: Calories 85 (Calories from Fat 20); Fat 3g (Saturated 0g); Cholesterol 0mg; Sodium 170mg; Carbohydrate 7g (Dietary Fiber 2g); Protein 11g • **% Daily Value:** Vitamin A 26%; Vitamin C 12%; Calcium 6%; Iron 16% • **Diet Exchanges:** 1 1/2 Very Lean Meat, 1 Vegetable

mediterranean eggs

baked egg casserole

good 2 know Ten-ounce custard cups are very convenient for baking individual servings. But if you don't have any, you can also bake this homey casserole in an 8 1/2 × 4 1/2 × 2 1/2-inch loaf pan.

prep 20 min • **bake** 25 min

1 cup garlic-flavored croutons

2 hard-cooked eggs, cut into halves

1 cup fresh or frozen (thawed and drained) broccoli cuts

1/2 cup shredded mozzarella cheese (2 ounces)

1 tablespoon butter or margarine

1 tablespoon all-purpose flour

1 teaspoon prepared horseradish

1/8 teaspoon pepper

1 1/4 cups milk

2 tablespoons grated Parmesan cheese

1. Heat oven to 350°. Arrange croutons evenly in 2 ungreased 10-ounce custard cups. Arrange egg halves and broccoli over croutons. Sprinkle with mozzarella cheese.

2. Heat butter in 1-quart saucepan over medium heat until melted. Stir in flour, horseradish and pepper. Cook, stirring constantly, until smooth and bubbly; remove from heat. Stir in milk. Heat to boiling, stirring constantly. Boil and stir 1 minute. Pour evenly over mozzarella cheese.

3. Sprinkle with Parmesan cheese. Bake uncovered 20 to 25 minutes or until sauce is bubbly and center is hot.

1 Serving: Calories 415 (Calories from Fat 205); Fat 23g (Saturated 12g); Cholesterol 255mg; Sodium 700mg; Carbohydrate 27g (Dietary Fiber 2g); Protein 26g • **% Daily Value:** Vitamin A 30%; Vitamin C 36%; Calcium 54%; Iron 10% • **Diet Exchanges:** 1 Starch, 2 High-Fat Meat, 1 Skim Milk, 1 Fat

eggs benedict

good 2 know Here's a great idea: use your microwave to make two tricky recipes—poaching eggs and making hollandaise sauce—easy, quick and foolproof! Just make sure to use butter for the sauce because margarine will not work.

prep 10 min • **microwave** 6 min • **stand** 3 min

Hollandaise Sauce (below)

4 slices Canadian-style bacon (1/8 inch thick)

1/4 cup hot water

1/2 teaspoon vinegar

2 eggs

1 English muffin, split and toasted

1. Prepare Hollandaise Sauce. Keep warm.

2. Place Canadian-style bacon on plate. Cover with waxed paper and microwave on High (100%) until hot, 45 to 60 seconds.

3. Divide water and vinegar between two 6-ounce custard cups. Cover tightly and microwave on High (100%) until boiling, 30 to 60 seconds. Break eggs into cups; pierce yolks with wooden pick. Cover tightly and microwave on Medium (50%) until desired doneness, 1 1/2 to 2 1/2 minutes; drain.

4. Place English muffin halves on plates; top with bacon and eggs. Serve with Hollandaise Sauce.

hollandaise sauce

3 tablespoons butter*

1 tablespoon lemon juice

1 tablespoon plus 1 teaspoon water

1 egg yolk

Place butter in 1-cup measure. Microwave uncovered on High (100%) just until melted, 30 to 45 seconds. Add lemon juice and water. Beat in egg yolk with fork. Microwave uncovered on Medium (50%), stirring every 15 seconds, until thickened, 45 seconds to 1 1/2 minutes. Do not overheat or sauce will curdle. Cover and let stand 3 minutes. Sauce will thicken as it stands. Cover and refrigerate any remaining sauce.

Do not use margarine in this recipe.

1 Serving: Calories 395 (Calories from Fat 260); Fat 29g (Saturated 14g); Cholesterol 390mg; Sodium 960mg; Carbohydrate 15g (Dietary Fiber 1g); Protein 20g • **% Daily Value:** Vitamin A 22%; Vitamin C 0%; Calcium 10%; Iron 10% • **Diet Exchanges:** 1 Starch, 2 1/2 High-Fat Meat, 2 Fat

cheesy asparagus frittata

The best way to remove the tough ends of the asparagus is to break them off as far down as the stalks snap easily.

prep 10 min • **cook** 16 min

4 eggs

1/4 cup milk

3/4 teaspoon chopped fresh or 1/4 teaspoon dried chervil leaves

1/8 teaspoon salt

1/2 cup shredded Swiss or Havarti cheese (2 ounces)

2 tablespoons butter or margarine

3/4 cup fresh or frozen asparagus, cut and thawed

1 clove garlic, finely chopped

1/4 cup chopped seeded tomato

1. Beat eggs, milk, chervil and salt in medium bowl until blended. Stir in cheese. Heat butter in 8-inch ovenproof skillet over medium heat until melted. Cook asparagus and garlic in butter about 3 minutes, stirring occasionally, until asparagus is crisp-tender. Stir in tomato; reduce heat to medium-low.

2. Pour egg mixture over vegetables. Cover and cook about 9 minutes, without stirring, until eggs are set almost to center and are light brown on bottom. Remove cover.

3. Set oven control to broil. Broil frittata with top about 5 inches from heat about 2 minutes or until eggs are completely set and just starting to brown.

1 Serving: Calories 335 (Calories from Fat 280); Fat 31g (Saturated 16g); Cholesterol 485mg; Sodium 440mg; Carbohydrate 7g (Dietary Fiber 1g); Protein 23g • **% Daily Value:** Vitamin A 38%; Vitamin C 12%; Calcium 36%; Iron 8% • **Diet Exchanges:** 3 High-Fat Meat, 1 Vegetable

cheesy asparagus frittata

french omelet with glazed apples

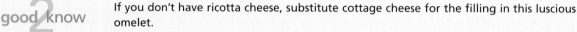

good 2 know   If you don't have ricotta cheese, substitute cottage cheese for the filling in this luscious omelet.

prep 10 min • **cook** 10 min • *photograph on page 157*

2 tablespoons packed brown sugar

2 tablespoons and 1 teaspoon butter or margarine

1 large unpeeled red apple, sliced

1/3 cup ricotta cheese

1/3 cup shredded Cheddar cheese (1 1/2 ounces)

4 eggs

2 tablespoons milk

1. Heat brown sugar and 1 tablespoon butter to boiling in 1 1/2-quart saucepan; reduce heat to medium. Stir in apple. Cook about 3 minutes, stirring frequently, until apple is crisp-tender. Remove from heat; keep warm. Mix ricotta cheese and Cheddar cheese. Beat eggs and milk in medium bowl.

2. Make 1 omelet at a time: Heat 2 teaspoons of remaining butter in 8-inch omelet pan or skillet over medium-high heat just until butter is hot and sizzling. As butter melts, tilt pan to coat bottom. Quickly pour half of the egg mixture into pan. While rapidly sliding pan back and forth over heat, quickly stir with fork to spread eggs continuously over bottom of pan as they thicken. Let stand over heat a few seconds to lightly brown bottom of omelet. Do not overcook—omelet will continue to cook after folding.

3. Tilt pan and run fork under edge of omelet, then jerk pan sharply to loosen eggs from bottom of pan. Spoon half of the cheese mixture down center of omelet. Fold portion of omelet just to center. Allow for a portion of the omelet to slide up side of pan. Turn omelet onto warm plate, flipping folded portion of omelet over so it rolls over the bottom. Tuck sides of omelet under if necessary. Spoon half of the apple slices over omelet.

4. Repeat with remaining 2 teaspoons butter, egg mixture, cheese mixture and apple slices.

1 Serving: Calories 485 (Calories from Fat 270); Fat 30g (Saturated 15g); Cholesterol 485mg; Sodium 370mg; Carbohydrate 34g (Dietary Fiber 3g); Protein 23g • **% Daily Value:** Vitamin A 28%; Vitamin C 4%; Calcium 30%; Iron 10% • **Diet Exchanges:** 3 High-Fat Meat, 2 Fruit, 1 1/2 Fat

easy huevos rancheros

good 2 know

Huevos Rancheros ("ranch-style eggs") refers to any egg dish served on tortillas. If you prefer, you can fry the eggs instead of poaching them.

prep 5 min • **cook** 18 min

2 flour tortillas (6 inches in diameter)

1 can (8 ounces) tomato sauce

1/4 cup salsa

1/4 teaspoon sugar

1/4 teaspoon ground cumin

1 clove garlic, finely chopped

4 eggs

1/4 cup shredded Colby-Monterey Jack cheese (1 ounce)

1. Heat oven to 350°. Wrap tortillas in aluminum foil. Heat about 10 minutes until warm. Remove tortillas from oven; keep wrapped.

2. Meanwhile, mix tomato sauce, salsa, sugar, cumin and garlic in 1-quart saucepan. Heat to boiling; reduce heat. Cover and simmer 5 minutes, stirring occasionally.

3. Heat water (1 1/2 to 2 inches) to boiling in 10-inch skillet; reduce heat to low. Break each egg, one at a time, into custard cup or saucer. Hold cup or saucer close to water's surface and slip egg into water. Cook uncovered 6 to 7 minutes or until whites are set and yolks are thickened. Remove eggs with slotted spoon.

4. Place each warm tortilla on dinner plate. Top each tortilla with 2 poached eggs and the sauce. Sprinkle with cheese.

table for 2

There's nothing better for a lazy day brunch on the porch than these Huevos Rancheros with a glass of fresh-squeezed orange juice and warm muffins. Try Tex-Mex Corn Muffins (page 155) or pick up muffins, scones or biscuits at your favorite bakery.

1 Serving: Calories 390 (Calories from Fat 170); Fat 19g (Saturated 7g); Cholesterol 440mg; Sodium 1300mg; Carbohydrate 37g (Dietary Fiber 4g); Protein 22g • **% Daily Value:** Vitamin A 34%; Vitamin C 16%; Calcium 20%; Iron 22% • **Diet Exchanges:** 2 Starch, 2 High-Fat Meat, 1 Vegetable

southwestern corn cakes

Like a meatless version of this easy breakfast cake? Replace the sausage links with 1/2 cup cooked pinto beans.

prep 8 min • bake 25 min • cool 10 min

1/2 cup frozen corn, broccoli and red pepper mixture, thawed

1 tablespoon sliced ripe olives

2 cooked pork sausage links (2 ounces), chopped

1 cup low-fat (skim) milk

1/4 cup fat-free cholesterol-free egg product or 1 egg white

1/3 cup Original Bisquick

2 tablespoons yellow cornmeal

1/2 teaspoon chili powder

1/4 cup chunky salsa, if desired

Cilantro, if desired

1. Heat oven to 425°. Spray two 10- to 12-ounce individual casseroles or custard cups with cooking spray.

2. Spoon half the corn mixture, olives and sausage into each casserole. Place milk, egg product, baking mix, cornmeal and chili powder in blender. Cover and blend on high speed 15 seconds or until smooth. (Or beat on high speed 1 minute.) Pour evenly over sausage mixture.

3. Bake uncovered 20 to 25 minutes or until knife inserted in center comes out clean. Cool 10 minutes. Top with salsa and cilantro.

1 Serving: Calories 315 (Calories from Fat 145); Fat 16g (Saturated 6g); Cholesterol 30mg; Sodium 700mg; Carbohydrate 30g (Dietary Fiber 2g); Protein 15g • **% Daily Value:** Vitamin A 28%; Vitamin C 24%; Calcium 22%; Iron 12% • **Diet Exchanges:** 2 Starch, 1 High-Fat Meat, 1 Fat

vegetable rarebit cups

good 2 know You can buy prebaked pastry shells at a bakery or unbaked shells in the frozen foods section of your supermarket. Follow the directions on the package to bake. Then fill the shells with this cheesy and zesty vegetable sauce for a lovely brunch entrée or a light supper.

prep 8 min • **cook** 12 min

2 cups frozen mixed broccoli, cauliflower and carrots

2 tablespoons butter or margarine

2 tablespoons all-purpose flour

1 teaspoon Dijon mustard

3/4 cup milk

2 tablespoons dry white wine or chicken broth

1 cup shredded Fontina or Cheddar cheese (4 ounces)

2 baked puff pastry shells

1. Cook vegetables as directed on package; drain well.

2. Heat butter in 1 1/2-quart saucepan over medium heat until melted. Stir in flour and mustard. Cook over medium heat, stirring constantly, until smooth and bubbly; remove from heat. Stir in milk. Heat to boiling, stirring constantly. Boil and stir 1 minute. Stir in wine. Gradually stir in cheese until melted. Fold in vegetables.

3. Serve cheese sauce over pastry shells.

1 Serving: Calories 640 (Calories from Fat 415); Fat 46g (Saturated 25g); Cholesterol 140mg; Sodium 670mg; Carbohydrate 36g (Dietary Fiber 3g); Protein 23g • **% Daily Value:** Vitamin A 78%; Vitamin C 26%; Calcium 56%; Iron 16% • **Diet Exchanges:** 2 Starch, 2 High-Fat Meat, 1 Vegetable, 6 Fat

mushroom quiches

Be sure to use deep (about 1 inch) quiche dishes or tart pans so all the filling fits in the pastry shell. If you prefer a vegetarian dish, just leave out the pepperoni.

prep 10 min • **bake** 45 min • **stand** 5 min

Easy Pastry (below)

1/2 cup shredded mozzarella cheese (2 ounces)

1/2 cup sliced mushrooms (about 1 1/2 ounces)

2 tablespoons chopped green bell pepper

1 tablespoon chopped pepperoni

1 egg

1/2 cup milk

2 tablespoons grated Parmesan cheese

1 teaspoon chopped fresh or 1/4 teaspoon dried basil leaves

1. Heat oven to 350°. Prepare Easy Pastry. Divide pastry into halves. Pat pastry firmly and evenly on bottoms and completely up sides of 2 deep individual 4-inch quiche dishes or tart pans or ungreased 10-ounce custard cups. Bake 15 to 20 minutes or until light brown.

2. Meanwhile, mix mozzarella cheese, mushrooms, bell pepper and pepperoni. Divide cheese mixture between baked crusts. Beat egg lightly in small bowl. Beat in remaining ingredients; pour into crusts.

3. Bake quiches about 25 minutes or until knife inserted in center comes out clean. Let stand 5 minutes before serving.

easy pastry

2/3 cup all-purpose flour

1/4 cup (1/2 stick) butter or margarine, softened

1 egg yolk

Mix all ingredients until flour is well blended. Gather pastry into a ball.

1 Serving: Calories 580 (Calories from Fat 340); Fat 38g (Saturated 22g); Cholesterol 300mg; Sodium 560mg; Carbohydrate 38g (Dietary Fiber 2g); Protein 23g • **% Daily Value:** Vitamin A 30%; Vitamin C 8%; Calcium 40%; Iron 16% • **Diet Exchanges:** 2 Starch, 2 High-Fat Meat, 1 Vegetable, 4 1/2 Fat

mushroom quiches

pancake and "sausage" stacks

good 2 know Waffles work just as well as pancakes for this recipe. Make homemade waffles, if you have the time, or keep it quick by using frozen waffles.

prep 10 min • **cook** 10 min

4 frozen vegetable and grain protein breakfast patties or sausage patties

1 medium cooking apple, chopped (about 1 cup)

1/2 cup maple-flavored syrup

1/4 teaspoon ground cinnamon

4 packaged frozen pancakes

1. Prepare patties as directed on package.

2. While patties are cooking, mix apples, syrup and cinnamon in 10-inch nonstick skillet. Heat to boiling; reduce heat to medium. Cook about 5 minutes, stirring occasionally, until apples are tender.

3. Prepare pancakes as directed on package.

4. For each serving, place 2 patties on 1 pancake; spoon apple mixture over patties. Top with additional pancake and apple mixture.

table for 2

To turn this everyday breakfast into an extra-indulgent treat, make homemade pancakes and stir 1/2 cup chopped apple and chopped nuts into the batter. Fresh orange juice, steaming hot coffee or tea are favorite beverages—or try a fruit smoothie for a delicious change.

1 Serving: Calories 560 (Calories from Fat 80); Fat 9g (Saturated 2g); Cholesterol 10mg; Sodium 950mg; Carbohydrate 1030g (Dietary Fiber 4g); Protein 21g • **% Daily Value:** Vitamin A 2%; Vitamin C 2%; Calcium 6%; Iron 18% • **Diet Exchanges:** 5 Starch, 1 Very Lean Meat, 2 Fruit

sunflower nut oven french toast

 good 2 know
This delicious oven French toast is sweetened with apple juice concentrate. Just scoop it out of the can and use it undiluted—it thaws in seconds as you mix it with other ingredients.

prep 7 min • bake 13 min

1 1/2 teaspoons vegetable oil

2 tablespoons chopped roasted unsalted sunflower nuts

3 tablespoons unsweetened frozen (thawed) apple juice concentrate

1/4 cup fat-free cholesterol-free egg product or 1 egg

4 slices 12-grain or other multigrain bread

1. Heat oven to 450°. Spread oil evenly in jelly roll pan, 15 1/2 × 10 1/2 × 1 inch, in area the size of 4 slices bread. Sprinkle 2 to 3 teaspoons sunflower nuts evenly over oil.

2. Beat apple juice concentrate and egg product with hand beater until blended. Dip bread into egg mixture; place in pan. Drizzle any remaining egg mixture over bread. Sprinkle remaining sunflower nuts evenly over bread. Bake 10 to 13 minutes or until bottoms are golden brown.

1 Serving: Calories 280 (Calories from Fat 110); Fat 12g (Saturated 2g); Cholesterol 0mg; Sodium 30mg; Carbohydrate 37g (Dietary Fiber 5g); Protein 11g • **% Daily Value:** Vitamin A 0%; Vitamin C 0%; Calcium 6%; Iron 14% • **Diet Exchanges:** 2 Starch, 1 Lean Meat, 1/2 Fruit, 1 Fat

peach oven pancake

good 2 know
Give this Sunday morning favorite new life throughout the year by using your favorite seasonal fruit. It's great with berries, bananas or cooked apples.

prep 10 min • Bake 20 min

1/3 cup all-purpose flour

1 teaspoon sugar

1/4 teaspoon salt

1/3 cup low-fat milk

2 eggs

1/2 cup vanilla yogurt

2 medium fresh peaches, peeled and sliced, or 2 cups frozen sliced peaches, thawed and drained

2 tablespoons high-fiber cereal, crushed, if desired

1. Heat oven to 400°. Spray round nonstick baking pan, 8 × 1 1/2 inches or 9 × 1 1/2 inches, with cooking spray. Heat pan in oven.

2. Beat flour, sugar, salt, milk and eggs with hand beater until smooth. Pour into hot pan.

3. Bake 15 to 20 minutes or until puffed and browned on edges. Immediately spoon yogurt and peaches into sunken pancake center; sprinkle with cereal. Serve warm.

1 Serving: Calories 305 (Calories from Fat 65); Fat 7g (Saturated 2g); Cholesterol 215mg; Sodium 410mg; Carbohydrate 51g (Dietary Fiber 4g); Protein 14g • **% Daily Value:** Vitamin A 14%; Vitamin C 10%; Calcium 18%; Iron 10% • **Diet Exchanges:** 1 1/2 Starch, 1 1/2 Lean Meat, 2 Fruit

peach oven pancake

carrot-potato patties

good 2 know If you like, offer a few different topping choices for these pleasing patties such as apple-sauce, sour cream or sour cream mixed with chopped chives or prepared horseradish.

prep 10 min • **cook** 6 min

1 1/2 medium carrots, shredded (1 cup)

1 medium potato, peeled and shredded (1 cup)

2 tablespoons grated onion

1/2 teaspoon salt

1/4 cup fat-free cholesterol-free egg product or 1 egg

1/4 cup unsweetened applesauce

1. Mix all ingredients, except applesauce, in medium bowl.

2. Spray nonstick griddle or 10-inch skillet with cooking spray. Heat griddle over medium heat or to 375°.

3. For each patty, spoon approximately 1/2 cup batter onto hot griddle. Cook 2 to 3 minutes on each side or until golden brown. Top warm patties with applesauce.

1 Serving: Calories 90 (Calories from Fat 0); Fat 0g (Saturated 0g); Cholesterol 0mg; Sodium 650mg; Carbohydrate 22g (Dietary Fiber 3g); Protein 4g • **% Daily Value:** Vitamin A 100%; Vitamin C 8%; Calcium 2%; Iron 6% • **Diet Exchanges:** 1 Vegetable, 1 Fruit

cinnamon-orange breakfast puffs

 good 2 know

If you like, you can also make regular-size muffins. The batter will fill 4 to 5 regular muffin cups. Bake about 20 minutes.

prep 15 min • **bake** 15 min • **cool** 5 min • **makes** 12 puffs

1 tablespoon plus 1 teaspoon
sugar

1/4 cup orange juice

2 teaspoons vegetable oil

1/2 teaspoon almond extract

2 tablespoons fat-free
cholesterol-free egg product
or 1 egg white

2/3 cup all-purpose flour

1 teaspoon baking powder

3/4 teaspoon ground
cinnamon

1/4 teaspoon grated
orange peel

3 tablespoons sugar

2 teaspoons butter or
margarine, melted

1. Heat oven to 400°. Spray 12 small muffin cups, 1 3/4 × 1 inch, with cooking spray.

2. Mix 1 tablespoon plus 1 teaspoon sugar, the orange juice, oil, almond extract and egg product in small bowl until well blended. Add flour, baking powder, 1/4 teaspoon cinnamon and the orange peel; stir just until moistened. Fill muffin cups 3/4 full.

3. Bake 12 to 15 minutes or until light brown. Remove from pan; cool 5 minutes. Mix 3 tablespoons sugar and remaining 1/2 teaspoon cinnamon in small bowl. Brush each puff with butter; roll in sugar-cinnamon mixture.

1 Puff: Calories 55 (Calories from Fat 10); Fat 1g (Saturated 0g); Cholesterol 0mg; Sodium 55mg; Carbohydrate 11g (Dietary Fiber 0g); Protein 1g • **% Daily Value:** Vitamin A 0%; Vitamin C 0%; Calcium 2%; Iron 2% • **Diet Exchanges:** 1 Fruit

caramel-pecan coffee cake

How would you like to have a fresh-baked coffee cake, dripping with brown sugar caramel and pecans, on the table in less than 15 minutes? Here's the secret: use your microwave! It really is possible—and it's incredibly delicious too!

prep 5 min • **microwave** 7 min • **stand** 1 min

2 tablespoons butter or margarine

1/4 cup packed brown sugar

2 tablespoons chopped pecans

2 tablespoons light corn syrup

1/4 teaspoon ground cinnamon

1 cup Original Bisquick

1/4 cup cold water

1. Place butter in 1-quart casserole. Microwave uncovered on High (100%) until melted, 20 to 30 seconds. Stir in brown sugar, pecans, corn syrup and cinnamon; spread evenly in casserole. Microwave uncovered until bubbly, 45 to 60 seconds. Tilt casserole so brown sugar mixture runs to side; place 6-ounce juice glass in center of casserole.

2. Mix Bisquick and water until soft dough forms. Drop dough by 6 spoonfuls onto brown sugar mixture. Place casserole on inverted plate in microwave oven. Microwave uncovered on Medium-high (70%) 2 minutes; rotate casserole 1/2 turn. Microwave uncovered until wooden pick inserted in center comes out clean, 2 to 2 1/2 minutes longer.

3. Remove glass. Immediately invert on heatproof serving plate; let casserole stand 1 minute so caramel can drizzle over coffee cake. Serve warm.

1 Serving: Calories 560 (Calories from Fat 225); Fat 25g (Saturated 10g); Cholesterol 30mg; Sodium 960mg; Carbohydrate 80g (Dietary Fiber 1g); Protein 5g • **% Daily Value:** Vitamin A 8%; Vitamin C 0%; Calcium 12%; Iron 14% • **Diet Exchanges:** 2 Starch, 3 Fruit, 5 Fat

caramel-pecan coffee cake

blueberry bran muffins

good 2 know Instant oatmeal products are not the same as quick-cooking and should not be used for baking—you will get gummy or mushy results.

prep 10 min • **bake** 20 min • **makes** 6 muffins

1/4 cup wheat bran

3 tablespoons honey

2 teaspoons vegetable oil

1/4 cup boiling water

1/2 cup whole wheat or whole wheat blend flour

2 tablespoons quick oats

1 teaspoon baking powder

1/4 teaspoon salt

1/4 teaspoon ground cinnamon

2 tablespoons fat-free cholesterol-free egg product or 1 egg white

1/3 cup fresh or frozen (thawed and well drained) blueberries

1. Heat oven to 400°. Spray 6 medium muffin cups, 2 1/2 × 1 1/4 inches, with cooking spray.

2. Stir bran, honey, oil and water in medium bowl until blended. Let stand 2 minutes. Stir in flour, oats, baking powder, salt, cinnamon and egg product until just moistened. Fold in blueberries. Fill muffins cups 2/3 full.

3. Bake 15 to 20 minutes or until golden brown.

1 Muffin: Calories 100 (Calories from Fat 20); Fat 2g (Saturated 0g); Cholesterol 0mg; Sodium 190mg; Carbohydrate 20g (Dietary Fiber 3g); Protein 3g • **% Daily Value:** Vitamin A 0%; Vitamin C 0%; Calcium 4%; Iron 4% • **Diet Exchanges:** 1 Starch, 1/2 Fat

strawberry-mandarin smoothie

good 2 know Frozen orange juice concentrate may be substituted for the mandarin tangerine juice. Freeze any remaining juice concentrate in its container, tightly covered with plastic wrap and foil.

prep 10 min

1 1/4 cups sliced fresh or frozen (thawed) strawberries (8 ounces)

1/3 cup frozen (thawed) mandarin tangerine juice concentrate

1/2 cup fat-free vanilla yogurt

1/3 cup cold water

2 strawberries with leaves, if desired

1. Place 1 1/4 cup sliced strawberries, juice concentrate, yogurt and water in blender. Cover and blend on medium-high speed until smooth.

2. Pour into two 8-ounce glasses. Make a slit in strawberries; place on rim of glasses as garnish.

1 Serving: Calories 95 (Calories from Fat 10); Fat 1g (Saturated 0g); Cholesterol 0mg; Sodium 30mg; Carbohydrate 22g (Dietary Fiber 3g); Protein 3g • **% Daily Value:** Vitamin A 4%; Vitamin C 100%; Calcium 10%; Iron 6% • **Diet Exchanges:** 1 1/2 Fruit

solutions for 2

vary your veggies

You just can't eat too many vegetables! With such a range of flavors, colors and textures, vegetables add limitless variety to our diets. Garden-fresh, frozen or canned, vegetables are widely available at all supermarkets. For the peak of the crop, take advantage of seasonal fresh vegetable specials at the farmers' market or the supermarket. Then try some of these quick and easy ideas to dress up your veggies:

- **Perk up steamed veggies** by tossing them with a few tablespoons of your favorite prepared sauce or salad dressing. Some yummy combinations to try: broccoli with teriyaki sauce; corn with barbecue sauce; zucchini with creamy peppercorn dressing; carrots with honey Dijon dressing.

- **Make an easy cheesy sauce** for vegetables. Just before the veggies are done, drain them and stir in cheese spread. Cover and let stand a few minutes until heated through. Stir in a little milk if cheese is too thick.

- **Purchase packaged cleaned mixed greens**—half the package is just right for a tossed salad for two. For a different side dish, heat some vinaigrette dressing and toss with salad greens until they are wilted. Top with crumbled cooked bacon.

- **Jazz up coleslaw** with some tasty toppers: try nuts, sunflower seeds, chopped dried fruit or crunchy chow mein noodles. They'll keep their crunch if you mix them in right before serving.

- **Mix vegetables and beans** with rice or couscous and herbs or seasonings rather than eating them separately. For a quick Mexican dish, stir chopped tomato, green onion, shredded cheese and chilies into steamed rice; for a flavorful Moroccan side, mix drained canned garbanzo beans, golden raisins, chopped onion and a pinch of ground cumin into prepared couscous.

- **Add your favorite combination** of frozen mixed vegetables to cold pasta salads for color and flavor. It's an easy addition since frozen vegetables need only be thawed, not cooked.

- **Top baked sweet potatoes** or cooked winter squash and carrots with butter and sprinkle with brown sugar and your favorite spice—cinnamon, nutmeg, allspice or ginger.

chapter five

on the
sidelines

side dishes, breads and snacks

fat

buttercup squash with apples

good 2 know Sprinkle toasted sunflower seeds or chopped toasted pecans over the cooked squash for a crunchy treat!

prep 5 min • **bake** 40 min

1 small buttercup or other winter squash, cut in half, seeds and fibers removed (1 pound)

1/2 cup chopped tart apple

2 teaspoons packed brown sugar

2 teaspoons butter or margarine, softened

1/2 teaspoon lemon juice

Dash of ground nutmeg

1. Heat oven to 400°. Place squash halves cut sides up in ungreased rectangular baking dish, 11 × 7 × 1 1/2 inches.

2. Mix remaining ingredients; spoon into squash. Cover and bake 30 to 40 minutes or until squash in tender.

1 Serving: Calories 105 (Calories from Fat 45); Fat 5g (Saturated 3g); Cholesterol 10mg; Sodium 30mg; Carbohydrate 17g (Dietary Fiber 3g); Protein 1g • **% Daily Value:** Vitamin A 52%; Vitamin C 8%; Calcium 2%; Iron 2% • **Diet Exchanges:** 1 Fruit, 1 Fat

buttercup squash with apples

asparagus parmesan

good 2 know

Does fresh asparagus sound good? Use about 1 pound, cut into 1-inch pieces, in place of the frozen asparagus. Add lower stalk pieces to boiling water; boil uncovered 6 minutes. Add tips; cover and boil 4 minutes more or until crisp-tender.

cook 10 min

1 1/3 cup frozen cut asparagus

6 mushrooms, thinly sliced

2 teaspoons butter or margarine

1/8 teaspoon garlic powder

Freshly ground pepper

1 tablespoon grated Parmesan cheese

Cook asparagus as directed on package—except add mushrooms during last minute of cooking; drain. Stir in remaining ingredients.

1 Serving: Calories 100 (Calories from Fat 55); Fat 6g (Saturated 3g); Cholesterol 15mg; Sodium 90mg; Carbohydrate 8g (Dietary Fiber 3g); Protein 6g • **% Daily Value:** Vitamin A 24%; Vitamin C 26%; Calcium 6%; Iron 8% • **Diet Exchanges:** 2 Vegetable, 1 Fat

marinated broccoli and carrot salad

 **good 2 know** Any leftover veggies in the fridge? Go ahead and toss them into this sensational chilled salad. Then add a bit more dressing if you need to.

cook 12 min • **chill** 1 hr

1 1/2 cups broccoli flowerets

1/4 cup sliced carrot

1 large green onion, sliced

3 tablespoons Italian dressing

2 lettuce leaves

1. Heat 1 inch water to boiling in 1 1/2-quart saucepan. Add broccoli, carrot and onion. Cover and heat to boiling; reduce heat. Boil 10 to 12 minutes or until broccoli is crisp-tender; drain.

2. Toss vegetables with dressing. Cover and refrigerate about 1 hour or until chilled. Serve on lettuce leaves.

1 Serving: Calories 120 (Calories from Fat 90); Fat 10g (Saturated 1g); Cholesterol 5mg; Sodium 230mg; Carbohydrate 8g (Dietary Fiber 3g); Protein 3g • **% Daily Value:** Vitamin A 80%; Vitamin C 54%; Calcium 6%; Iron 6% • **Diet Exchanges:** 1 1/2 Vegetable, 2 Fat

sweet-and-sour cabbage slaw

 good 2 know   Pack up your favorite sandwich and this coleslaw and head out to the park or the beach. Since it's made without any mayonnaise, this version is perfect for the great outdoors!

prep 5 min

2 tablespoons honey

2 tablespoons peach or apricot spreadable fruit

2 teaspoons cider vinegar

2 cups coleslaw mixture or shredded cabbage

2 green onions, sliced

1 medium carrot, shredded (2/3 cup)

Mix honey, spreadable fruit and vinegar in medium bowl. Add remaining ingredients; toss.

1 Serving: Calories 145 (Calories from Fat 0); Fat 0g (Saturated 0g); Cholesterol 0mg; Sodium 30mg; Carbohydrate 38g (Dietary Fiber 4g); Protein 2g • **% Daily Value:** Vitamin A 100%; Vitamin C 50%; Calcium 6%; Iron 6% • **Diet Exchanges:** 1 Vegetable, 2 Fruit

super express | low fat

green beans and red peppers

 good 2 know   If you don't have honey mustard on hand, just stir honey a bit at a time into a scant table-spoon of Dijon mustard and taste until sweetened to your liking.

prep 4 min • **cook** 15 min

1/2 pound fresh green beans, broken into 2-inch pieces (2 cups)

1/2 medium red bell pepper, cut into 2 × 1/4-inch strips

1 tablespoon honey mustard

Place beans in 1 inch water in 1 1/2-quart saucepan. Heat to boiling; reduce heat. Boil, uncovered, 5 minutes. Cover and boil 5 to 10 minutes longer or until beans are crisp-tender; drain. Stir in bell pepper and honey mustard.

1 Serving: Calories 35 (Calories from Fat 0); Fat 0g (Saturated 0g); Cholesterol 0mg; Sodium 75mg; Carbohydrate 11g (Dietary Fiber 4g); Protein 2g • **% Daily Value:** Vitamin A 46%; Vitamin C 50%; Calcium 4%; Iron 6% • **Diet Exchanges:** 1 1/2 Vegetable

maple-glazed carrots and apples

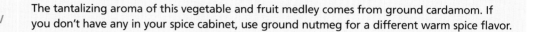

good2know The tantalizing aroma of this vegetable and fruit medley comes from ground cardamom. If you don't have any in your spice cabinet, use ground nutmeg for a different warm spice flavor.

prep 4 min • **cook** 15 min

2 medium carrots, sliced (1 cup)

1 tablespoon butter or margarine

1 medium apple, cut into thin wedges

2 tablespoons maple-flavored syrup

1/4 teaspoon ground cardamom

1. Heat 1 inch water (salted if desired) to boiling in 1-quart saucepan. Add carrots. Cover and heat to boiling; reduce heat. Simmer 12 to 15 minutes or until tender; drain.

2. While carrots are cooking, heat butter in 6-inch skillet over medium heat until hot. Cook apple wedges in butter 2 minutes, stirring occasionally. Stir in syrup and cardamom. Cook 3 to 5 minutes, stirring frequently, until apples are evenly glazed. Stir into carrots.

1 Serving: Calories 170 (Calories from Fat 55); Fat 6g (Saturated 4g); Cholesterol 15mg; Sodium 85mg; Carbohydrate 32g (Dietary Fiber 4g); Protein 1g • **% Daily Value:** Vitamin A 100%; Vitamin C 8%; Calcium 2%; Iron 2% • **Diet Exchanges:** 2 Fruit, 1 Fat

maple-glazed carrots and apples; cornish hen with bulgur (page 54)

peppery corn and tomatoes

A pinch of cayenne gives this side some feisty flair. It's a yummy accompaniment to crispy fried chicken.

cook 5 min

1 1/3 cups frozen whole kernel corn

1/4 cup garlic salt

Dash of ground red pepper (cayenne)

2 teaspoons butter or margarine

2 green onions, chopped

1/2 medium tomato, chopped

Cook corn as directed on package; drain. Stir in remaining ingredients.

1 Serving: Calories 130 (Calories from Fat 35); Fat 4g (Saturated 2g); Cholesterol 10mg; Sodium 160mg; Carbohydrate 23g (Dietary Fiber 3g); Protein 3g • **% Daily Value:** Vitamin A 12%; Vitamin C 10%; Calcium 2%; Iron 4% • **Diet Exchanges:** 1 Starch, 1 Vegetable, 1/2 Fat

southwestern corn salad

good 2 know This colorful, tasty salad makes a nice change from everyday salsa. Serve it just like salsa, spooned over your favorite burritos or scoop it up with tortilla chips.

prep 5 min • **cook** 5 min • **chill** 2 hr

3/4 cup spicy reduced-sodium vegetable juice

1/4 teaspoon chili powder

1/4 teaspoon ground cumin

1 1/2 cups frozen corn

1 small zucchini, cut into 1 × 1/4 × 1/4-inch sticks (1/2 cup)

1/4 teaspoon salt

2 lettuce leaves, if desired

Juice from 1/2 lime (about 2 teaspoons)

1. Heat vegetable juice, chili powder and cumin in 1 1/2-quart saucepan to boiling. Stir in corn and zucchini. Cover and cook over medium heat 3 to 5 minutes, stirring occasionally, until vegetables are tender. Stir in salt.

2. Cover and refrigerate about 2 hours or until chilled. Serve salad on lettuce leaves. Drizzle with lime juice.

1 Serving: Calories 130 (Calories from Fat 10); Fat 1g (Saturated 0g); Cholesterol 0mg; Sodium 320mg; Carbohydrate 29g (Dietary Fiber 4g); Protein 5g • **% Daily Value:** Vitamin A 40%; Vitamin C 58%; Calcium 2%; Iron 6% • **Diet Exchanges:** 1 Starch, 2 Vegetable

hawaiian yam casserole

good2know Crunchy with pecans, gooey with brown sugar and pineapple, this is just right for a holiday celebration meal.

prep 5 min • **bake** 45 min

2 medium sweet potatoes or yams, peeled and cut into 1/2-inch slices (about 2 cups)

1 can (8 ounces) crushed pineapple in juice, undrained

1 tablespoon packed brown sugar

2 tablespoons chopped pecans

1 tablespoon chopped crystallized ginger

1 teaspoon butter or margarine, softened

1. Heat oven to 375°. Spray 1-quart casserole with nonstick cooking spray.

2. Layer potatoes and crushed pineapple in casserole. Sprinkle brown sugar, pecans and crystallized ginger over top; dot with butter. Cover and bake about 45 minutes or until potatoes are tender.

1 Serving: Calories 280 (Calories from Fat 65); Fat 7g (Saturated 2g); Cholesterol 5mg; Sodium 30mg; Carbohydrate 56g (Dietary Fiber 5g); Protein 3g • **% Daily Value:** Vitamin A 100%; Vitamin C 32%; Calcium 6%; Iron 6% • **Diet Exchanges:** 2 Vegetable, 3 Fruit, 1 Fat

hurry-up potato salad

good 2 know Frozen hash brown potatoes mixed with onions and peppers make great potato salad— and a speedy shortcut when you're pressed for time.

prep 5 min • **cook** 8 min • **chill** 1 hr • *photograph on page 63*

2 cups frozen hash brown potatoes with onions and peppers

1/4 cup shredded carrot

1/4 cup sour cream

2 tablespoons mayonnaise or salad dressing

1/4 teaspoon curry powder

1/8 teaspoon salt

1/8 teaspoon ground mustard

1. Heat 1 inch water (salted if desired) to boiling in 1-quart saucepan. Add potatoes. Cover and heat to boiling; reduce heat. Simmer 6 to 8 minutes or until potatoes are tender; drain.

2. Mix remaining ingredients in medium glass or plastic bowl. Fold in potatoes. Cover and refrigerate at least 1 hour.

1 Serving: Calories 315 (Calories from Fat 155); Fat 17g (Saturated 5g); Cholesterol 25mg; Sodium 730mg; Carbohydrate 40g (Dietary Fiber 4g); Protein 4g • **% Daily Value:** Vitamin A 54%; Vitamin C 12%; Calcium 4%; Iron 4% • **Diet Exchanges:** 2 Starch, 1/2 Fruit, 3 Fat

baked potato with toppers

good 2 know Broccoli and bell pepper are just one delicious way to stuff baked spuds. Try any of the stuffing choices below—or offer your dining companion and yourself several choices!

prep 5 min • **bake** 55 min

2 large unpeeled baking
potatoes, such as russets
(about 8 ounces each)

1/4 cup reduced-fat sour cream

1/8 teaspoon garlic and
pepper seasoning blend

Dash of butter-flavor sprinkles

3/4 cup frozen broccoli,
cooked and drained

1 tablespoon chopped red
bell pepper

1. Heat oven to 400°. Scrub potatoes but do not peel. Prick potatoes with fork. Place in pie plate, 9 × 1 1/4 inches or 10 × 1 1/2 inches.

2. Bake potatoes 45 to 55 minutes. Slit tops of potatoes and squeeze open. Mix sour cream, seasoning blend and butter-flavor sprinkles. Spoon onto potatoes; top with broccoli and red peppers.

to microwave: Pierce potatoes to allow steam to escape. Arrange potatoes 1 inch apart on paper towel in microwave. Microwave uncovered on High (100%) 3 minutes; turn potatoes over. Microwave uncovered until tender, 3 1/2 to 5 minutes longer. Wrap potatoes in aluminum foil; let stand 5 minutes.

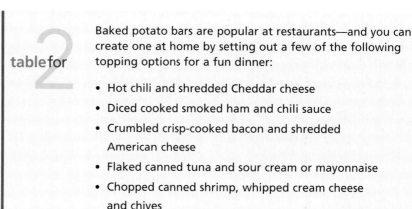

table for 2

Baked potato bars are popular at restaurants—and you can create one at home by setting out a few of the following topping options for a fun dinner:

• Hot chili and shredded Cheddar cheese

• Diced cooked smoked ham and chili sauce

• Crumbled crisp-cooked bacon and shredded American cheese

• Flaked canned tuna and sour cream or mayonnaise

• Chopped canned shrimp, whipped cream cheese and chives

1 Serving: Calories 240 (Calories from Fat 20); Fat 2g (Saturated 1g); Cholesterol 10mg; Sodium 60mg; Carbohydrate 54g (Dietary Fiber 7g); Protein 8g • **% Daily Value:** Vitamin A 32%; Vitamin C 50%; Calcium 8%; Iron 16% • **Diet Exchanges:** 3 Starch

baked potato with toppers; mango-lime cooler (page 174)

grilled vegetable kabobs

On those evenings when you don't feel like firing up the grill, these flavorful veggies will cook equally well under the broiler.

prep 8 min • **grill** 30 min

2 ten- or eleven-inch bamboo or metal skewers

1 teaspoon taco seasoning mix

1/4 cup Italian dressing

2 medium new potatoes, cut in half (1 to 1 1/2 inches in diameter)

1 small zucchini, cut in fourths

1 ear corn, cob broken or cut in fourths

1/2 bell pepper, cut in fourths

1. If using bamboo or wooden skewers, soak in water for 30 minutes before using to prevent burning. Heat grill. Mix taco seasoning and dressing. Thread remaining ingredients, alternating vegetables, on 2 skewers, leaving space between pieces. Brush dressing mixture over vegetables.

2. Cover and grill kabobs over medium coals 4 inches from heat 25 to 30 minutes, turning frequently and brushing with dressing, until vegetables are tender.

1 Serving: Calories 285 (Calories from Fat 115); Fat 13g (Saturated 1g); Cholesterol 5mg; Sodium 360mg; Carbohydrate 42g (Dietary Fiber 5g); Protein 5g • **% Daily Value:** Vitamin A 16%; Vitamin C 38%; Calcium 6%; Iron 10% • **Diet Exchanges:** 2 Starch, 2 Vegetable, 2 Fat

roasted fall vegetables

Roasting vegetables intensifies their flavors, and produces a crisp, dry surface. For a fresh, moist look, drizzle with additional salad dressing just before using.

prep 10 min • **roast** 20 min

4 ounces baby carrots, cut lengthwise in half (3/4 cup)

6 ounces butternut or acorn squash, peeled and cut into 3/4-inch cubes

1/2-pound leek, cut into pieces (1/2 cup)

5 small new potatoes, cut into 1-inch chunks (1/2 pound)

2 tablespoons honey-mustard dressing

2 teaspoons grated Parmesan cheese

1. Heat oven to 450°. Line jelly roll pan, 15 1/2 × 10 1/2 × 1 inch, with aluminum foil. Spray foil with cooking spray.

2. Mix carrots, squash, leek and potatoes with dressing until evenly coated. Place vegetables in single layer on foil. Sprinkle with cheese. Roast 20 minutes or until vegetables are tender.

1 Serving: Calories 220 (Calories from Fat 55); Fat 6g (Saturated 1g); Cholesterol 0mg; Sodium 170mg; Carbohydrate 43g (Dietary Fiber 6g); Protein 5g • **% Daily Value:** Vitamin A 100%; Vitamin C 28%; Calcium 10%; Iron 14% • **Diet Exchanges:** 2 Starch, 2 Vegetable, 1/2 Fat

sweet-and-sour vegetable stir-fry

good 2 know Crisp-tender vegetables in sweet-and-sour sauce are just right for dinner served over steamed rice or Asian noodles. Adding some shrimp or tofu to the mix makes it a little heartier.

prep 8 min • **cook** 6 min

1 tablespoon vegetable oil

1/2 cup sliced yellow summer squash or zucchini

1/2 cup sliced mushrooms (about 1 1/2 ounces)

4 green onions, cut diagonally into 1-inch pieces

1/2 cup Chinese pea pods

3 tablespoons prepared sweet-and-sour sauce

1 tablespoon water

1. Heat wok or 10-inch skillet over high heat until 1 or 2 drops of water bubble and skitter when sprinkled in wok. Add oil; rotate wok to coat side.

2. Add squash, mushrooms and onions; stir-fry about 3 minutes or until vegetables are crisp-tender. Add pea pods; stir-fry about 1 minute or until pea pods are crisp-tender. Stir in sweet-and-sour sauce and water. Cook and stir about 1 minute or until mixture is heated through.

1 Serving: Calories 100 (Calories from Fat 55); Fat 6g (Saturated 1g); Cholesterol 0mg; Sodium 95mg; Carbohydrate 12g (Dietary Fiber 2g); Protein 2g • **% Daily Value:** Vitamin A 6%; Vitamin C 14%; Calcium 4%; Iron 6% • **Diet Exchanges:** 2 Vegetable, 1 Fat

teriyaki spinach salad

good 2 know

This warm Asian-flavored salad, chockfull of vegetables, makes a wonderful lunch or light dinner when served with rice. Or serve it on the side with grilled chicken or fish.

prep 12 min

1 tablespoon stir-fry sauce
with garlic and ginger

1 teaspoon teriyaki sauce

1 teaspoon sweet-and-sour
sauce

4 cups fresh spinach leaves
(3 ounces)

2/3 cup canned baby corn,
rinsed and drained

1/2 cup sliced mushrooms

1 roma (plum) tomato,
chopped

1 tablespoon bacon-flavored
bits

1. Heat stir-fry, teriyaki and sweet-and-sour sauces in 10-inch skillet over medium heat, stirring constantly, about 1 minute or until hot and bubbly.

2. Add spinach, baby corn and mushrooms. Toss vegetables with dressing for about 1 minute or until well coated and spinach is wilted. Remove from heat; sprinkle with tomato and bacon-flavored bits.

1 Serving: Calories 100 (Calories from Fat 20); Fat 2g (Saturated 0g); Cholesterol 0mg; Sodium 700mg; Carbohydrate 18g (Dietary Fiber 4g); Protein 6g • **% Daily Value:** Vitamin A 100%; Vitamin C 44%; Calcium 8%; Iron 16% • **Diet Exchanges:** 3 Vegetable, 1/2 Fat

sesame vegetable medley

good 2 know

This extra-colorful assortment of vegetables looks terrific served alongside any dish with a rich, dark sauce. Try it with Turkey with Mushrooms and Wine (page 56) and wild rice for a celebratory dinner.

cook 10 min

1 1/2 cups frozen mixed broccoli, corn and peppers

1 tablespoon butter or margarine

2 teaspoons sesame seed

2 teaspoons lemon juice

1/4 teaspoon finely shredded lemon peel

1. Cook frozen vegetables as directed on package; drain.

2. Heat butter in 10-inch skillet over medium heat until melted. Cook sesame seed in butter about 5 minutes, stirring frequently, until golden brown; remove from heat. Stir in lemon juice and lemon peel; fold into vegetables.

1 Serving: Calories 130 (Calories from Fat 70); Fat 8g (Saturated 4g); Cholesterol 15mg; Sodium 60mg; Carbohydrate 13g (Dietary Fiber 3g); Protein 4g • **% Daily Value:** Vitamin A 30%; Vitamin C 32%; Calcium 4%; Iron 4% • **Diet Exchanges:** 3 Vegetable, 1 Fat

sesame vegetable medley; turkey with mushrooms and wine (page 56)

orange salad with blackberry dressing

 good 2 know | It's easy to turn this fruity salad into a hearty main dish for two—just add a bag of mixed salad greens and two sliced grilled chicken breast halves.

prep 12 min

2 small oranges, peeled and sliced

4 thin slices onion, separated into rings

2 tablespoons toasted slivered almonds

1/2 cup fresh or frozen (slightly thawed) blackberries

2 tablespoons almond or vegetable oil

1 tablespoon raspberry or white vinegar

1 tablespoon water

1/2 teaspoon sugar

1/8 teaspoon ground nutmeg

1. Arrange orange slices on 2 salad plates. Top with onion rings and sprinkle with almonds.

2. Place remaining ingredients in blender. Cover and blend until smooth. Serve dressing with salads.

1 Serving: Calories 245 (Calories from Fat 155); Fat 17g (Saturated 1g); Cholesterol 0mg; Sodium 0mg; Carbohydrate 26g (Dietary Fiber 6g); Protein 3g • **% Daily Value:** Vitamin A 8%; Vitamin C 100%; Calcium 8%; Iron 4% • **Diet Exchanges:** 2 Vegetable, 1 Fruit, 2 Fat

couscous pilaf

good2know
This flavorful medley makes three side-dish servings or two meatless main-dish servings. As a side, try it with broiled lamb chops rubbed with fresh or dried herbs.

prep 20 min • **bake** 20 min

3/4 cup uncooked couscous

1 cup chicken broth

1 tablespoon butter or margarine

3 ounces fresh mushrooms, chopped (1/2 cup)

1/4 cup chopped cashews or pecans

1/3 cup chopped green bell pepper

1 medium tomato, chopped (2/3 cup)

1/2 teaspoon ground nutmeg

1/2 teaspoon ground coriander

1/2 teaspoon garlic salt

2 green onions, chopped

1. Heat oven to 375°. Spray round nonstick baking pan, 9 × 1 1/2 inches, or square baking dish, 8 × 8 × 2 inches, with cooking spray.

2. Mix couscous and broth in pan; cover with aluminum foil. Bake 10 minutes; fluff with fork.

3. Meanwhile, heat butter in 10-inch nonstick skillet over medium-high heat. Sauté mushrooms, cashews and bell pepper until bell pepper is crisp-tender; remove from heat. Stir in remaining ingredients. Stir vegetable mixture into couscous in pan.

4. Bake pilaf, uncovered, 10 minutes longer or until couscous is slightly brown.

1 Serving: Calories 380 (Calories from Fat 145); Fat 16g (Saturated 6g); Cholesterol 15mg; Sodium 260mg; Carbohydrate 63g (Dietary Fiber 6g); Protein 15g • **% Daily Value:** Vitamin A 16%; Vitamin C 32%; Calcium 4%; Iron 16% • **Diet Exchanges:** 4 Starch, 1 Vegetable, 1 Fat

poppy seed fettuccine

For a festive side, toss in any chopped fresh herb like dill, parsley, chives or basil.

cook 12 min

4 ounces uncooked fettuccine

2 teaspoons butter or margarine

1/4 teaspoon poppy seed

Cook fettuccine as directed on package; drain. Stir in butter and poppy seed.

1 Serving: Calories 210 (Calories from Fat 55); Fat 6g (Saturated 3g); Cholesterol 60mg; Sodium 35mg; Carbohydrate 37g (Dietary Fiber 2g); Protein 7g • **% Daily Value:** Vitamin A 4%; Vitamin C 0%; Calcium 2%; Iron 12% • **Diet Exchanges:** 2 Starch, 1 Fat

spicy brown rice veracruz

good 2 know

This spicy brown rice dish can also double as the main dish in a meatless meal. Serve it in half of a baked acorn squash, topped with a small jalapeño chili. Add a piece of cornbread and a glass of low-fat milk.

prep 5 min • **cook** 10 min

1 teaspoon vegetable oil

3/4 cup instant brown rice

1 medium onion, chopped (1/2 cup)

2 cloves garlic, finely chopped

1 can (10 ounces) diced tomatoes with green chilies, undrained

1 can (8 ounces) tomato sauce

1/2 teaspoon chopped fresh jalapeño chilies, if desired

1. Heat oil in 10-inch nonstick skillet over medium-high heat. Cook rice, onion and garlic in oil 4 to 5 minutes, stirring frequently, until rice is toasted.

2. Stir in remaining ingredients, Cover and cook over medium-low heat 5 minutes or until rice is tender.

1 Serving: Calories 350 (Calories from Fat 45); Fat 5g (Saturated 1g); Cholesterol 0mg; Sodium 960mg; Carbohydrate 74g (Dietary Fiber 8g); Protein 10g • **% Daily Value:** Vitamin A 26%; Vitamin C 34%; Calcium 10%; Iron 16% • **Diet Exchanges:** 4 Starch, 2 Vegetable

warm biscuits

good 2 know Fresh, home-baked biscuits turn a simple meal into something extra-special! No need to save biscuits for a crowd—with Bisquick you can make just enough for the two of you!

prep 5 min • **bake** 10 min • **makes** 5 biscuits

1 1/4 cups Original Bisquick

1/2 cup milk

1. Heat oven to 450°. Stir ingredients until soft dough forms.

2. Turn onto surface dusted with Bisquick. Knead 10 times. Roll 1/2 inch thick. Cut with 2 1/2-inch cutter. Place on ungreased cookie sheet.

3. Bake 8 to 10 minutes or until golden brown.

1 Biscuit: Calories 135 (Calories from Fat 45); Fat 5g (Saturated 1g); Cholesterol 0mg; Sodium 440mg; Carbohydrate 19g (Dietary Fiber 0g); Protein 3g • **% Daily Value:** Vitamin A 0%; Vitamin C 0%; Calcium 8%; Iron 4% • **Diet Exchanges:** 1 Starch; 1 Fat

tex-mex corn muffins

good2know These muffins are the perfect accompaniment to soups and stews as well as to any south-western or southern-style meals.

prep 15 min • **bake** 20 min • **makes** 4 muffins

1/2 cup cornmeal

1/4 cup all-purpose flour

1/3 cup milk

2 tablespoons vegetable oil

3/4 teaspoon baking powder

1/8 teaspoon salt

1 egg

1/4 cup shredded hot pepper cheese (1 ounce)

2 teaspoons chopped fresh parsley

1. Heat oven to 450°. Grease bottoms only of 4 medium muffin cups, 2 1/2 × 1 1/4 inches.

2. Mix all ingredients except cheese and parsley in medium bowl; beat vigorously 30 seconds. Fold in cheese and parsley. Divide batter evenly among muffin cups.

3. Bake about 20 minutes or until golden. Immediately remove from pan. Serve warm.

1 Muffin: Calories 200 (Calories from Fat 100); Fat 11g (Saturated 3g); Cholesterol 60mg; Sodium 240mg; Carbohydrate 21g (Dietary Fiber 2g); Protein 6g • **% Daily Value:** Vitamin A 6%; Vitamin C 0%; Calcium 14%; Iron 8% • **Diet Exchanges:** 1 1/2 Starch, 2 Fat

orange-pecan muffins

good 2 know To toast pecans, sprinkle them in an ungreased heavy skillet. Cook over medium heat 4 to 6 minutes, stirring constantly, until golden brown and fragrant.

prep 20 min • **bake** 25 min • **makes** 4 muffins

1/3 cup orange juice

2 tablespoons packed brown sugar

2 tablespoons butter or margarine, melted

1 egg white

1/4 cup all-purpose flour

1/4 cup whole wheat flour

1 teaspoon baking powder

1/4 teaspoon grated orange peel

2 tablespoons finely chopped toasted pecans

1. Heat oven to 400°. Grease bottoms only of 4 medium muffin cups, 2 1/2 × 1 1/4 inches, or line with paper baking cups.

2. Beat orange juice, brown sugar, butter and egg white in medium bowl. Stir in flours, baking powder and orange peel all at once just until flour is moistened (batter will be lumpy). Fold in pecans. Divide batter evenly among muffin cups.

3. Bake 20 to 25 minutes or until golden brown. Immediately remove from pan.

1 Muffin: Calories 175 (Calories from Fat 80); Fat 9g (Saturated 4g); Cholesterol 16mg; Sodium 180mg; Carbohydrate 21g (Dietary Fiber 1g); Protein 3g • **% Daily Value:** Vitamin A 4%; Vitamin C 6%; Calcium 8%; Iron 6% • **Diet Exchanges:** 1 1/2 Starch, 1 1/2 Fat

orange-pecan muffins; french omelet with glazed apples (page 112)

mediterranean bread crisps

Kalamata olives are purple-colored Greek olives with a briny, fruity flavor. If you buy olives at the deli, you can often taste one or two varieties before choosing the kind you prefer.

prep 5 min • **bake** 10 min

1 tablespoon butter or margarine, softened

1 tablespoon crumbled feta cheese

4 thin slices French bread

1 tablespoon chopped Greek or ripe olives

1. Heat oven to 400°.

2. Mix butter and cheese; spread over bread. Sprinkle with olives. Place on ungreased cookie sheet. Bake about 10 minutes or until crisp.

1 Crisp: Calories 75 (Calories from Fat 35); Fat 4g (Saturated 2g); Cholesterol 10mg; Sodium 150mg; Carbohydrate 8g (Dietary Fiber 0g); Protein 2g • **% Daily Value:** Vitamin A 2%; Vitamin C 0%; Calcium 2%; Iron 2% • **Diet Exchanges:** 1/2 Starch, 1 Fat

sesame fingers

good 2 know

Here's a delicious way to dress up sliced bread. Serve these crunchy bites alongside anything good for dipping, such as salsa, soup or salad.

broil 2 min • *photograph on page 93*

2 tablespoons butter or margarine, softened

4 slices whole wheat bread

2 teaspoons sesame seed

1. Set oven control to broil.

2. Spread butter over bread. Sprinkle with sesame seed. Cut each slice into 4 strips. Place strips on rack in broiler pan. Broil 4 inches from heat 1 1/2 to 2 minutes or until edges of bread are brown.

4 Strips: Calories 130 (Calories from Fat 70); Fat 8g (Saturated 4g); Cholesterol 15mg; Sodium 170mg; Carbohydrate 12g (Dietary Fiber 1g); Protein 3g • **% Daily Value:** Vitamin A 4%; Vitamin C 0%; Calcium 2%; Iron 4% • **Diet Exchanges:** 1 Starch, 1 Fat

solutions for

2

delightful desserts

Don't desert desserts! Even on days when you don't plan to make or bake dessert, there are lots of light, fruity and tasty treats to enjoy. Here are ten easy and delicious dessert ideas to try:

- **Sliced strawberries** topped with a mixture of whipped topping and finely chopped fresh mint leaves.

- **Sliced peaches** topped with raspberry yogurt and crunchy granola.

- **Seedless green grapes** topped with vanilla yogurt and sprinkled with a little brown sugar.

- **Fresh pineapple slices** drizzled with rum or apple juice and sprinkled with finely chopped crystallized ginger and toasted shredded coconut.

- **Angel food cake** topped with lemon yogurt and fresh raspberries.

- **Gingersnaps or graham crackers** spread with plain or whipped cream cheese and topped with sliced pears or apples.

- **Vanilla frozen yogurt** topped with maple-flavored syrup and crunchy granola.

- **Orange frozen yogurt** topped with crumbled gingersnaps.

- **Tart apple** thinly sliced and topped with vanilla frozen yogurt, caramel ice cream topping and chopped toasted nuts.

- **Pound cake** topped with chocolate chips and miniature marshmallows, broiled about 5 inches from heat about 1 minute or until marshmallows are golden.

sweet
endings

simply desserts

chocolate and vanilla swirl pudding

good 2 know

Here's a dessert that offers the best of both worlds: a half vanilla and half chocolate swirled pudding. But if you're a die-hard chocolate fan, just double the amount of chocolate and add it to all of the pudding!

microwave 4 min • **chill** 1 hr

2 tablespoons sugar

1 tablespoon cornstarch

1 cup milk

2 tablespoons beaten egg

1 1/2 teaspoons butter or margarine

1/2 teaspoon vanilla

1 tablespoon semisweet chocolate chips

Fresh berries or sliced almonds, if desired

1. Mix sugar and cornstarch in 2-cup measure; stir in milk and egg. Microwave uncovered on High (100%) 2 minutes; stir. Microwave uncovered until mixture thickens and boils, 1 1/2 to 2 minutes longer; stir in butter and vanilla.

2. Transfer half of pudding to another bowl and stir in chocolate until melted and smooth. Layer vanilla and chocolate pudding alternately in parfait glasses or swirl in serving dish. Cover and refrigerate about 1 hour or until chilled. Serve topped with berries or almonds.

table for 2

For a dinner that's just like Grandma used to make, serve meatloaf (like Vegetable-Turkey Loaf, page 57) with creamy mashed potatoes and buttered peas. This swirled pudding is the perfect finale!

1 Serving: Calories 200 (Calories from Fat 70); Fat 8g (Saturated 5g); Cholesterol 80mg; Sodium 100mg; Carbohydrate 25g (Dietary Fiber 0g); Protein 6g • **% Daily Value:** Vitamin A 8%; Vitamin C 0%; Calcium 16%; Iron 2% • **Diet Exchanges:** 1 Fruit, 1 Skim Milk, 1 Fat

chocolate and vanilla swirl pudding

honey-spice apple

You can also top warm apples with a spoonful of vanilla yogurt for an energizing breakfast. Tart apples, like Rome, Greening or Granny Smith, are best for this simple dessert.

prep 5 min • **microwave** 4 min

2 medium unpeeled cooking apples

2 tablespoons raisins

2 tablespoons honey

1/4 teaspoon ground cinnamon

2 teaspoons butter or margarine

Heavy cream, if desired

1. Core apples to within 1/2 inch of bottom. Peel 1 inch of skin from around middle of each apple to prevent splitting. Place apples in two 10-ounce custard cups.

2. Pack raisins into apples. Mix honey and cinnamon; pour over raisins into apples. Top with butter.

3. Cover tightly and microwave on High (100%) until tender when pierced with fork, 3 to 4 minutes. Serve warm with cream.

1 Serving: Calories 210 (Calories from Fat 35); Fat 4g (Saturated 2g); Cholesterol 10mg; Sodium 25mg; Carbohydrate 46g (Dietary Fiber 4g); Protein 1g • **% Daily Value:** Vitamin A 4%; Vitamin C 6%; Calcium 2%; Iron 2% • **Diet Exchanges:** 3 Fruit, 1/2 Fat

apple crisp

good 2 know There really is a way to have home-baked apple crisp in less than 15 minutes. The secret is your microwave! Try topping the crisp with cinnamon ice cream for a sensational taste treat.

prep 7 min • **microwave** 6 min • *photograph on page 6*

1 1/2 cups sliced tart apples

2 tablespoons all-purpose flour

2 tablespoons quick-cooking oats

2 tablespoons packed brown sugar

2 tablespoons butter or margarine, softened

1/8 teaspoon ground cinnamon

1/8 teaspoon ground nutmeg

Vanilla or cinnamon ice cream, if desired

1. Spread apple slices in 24-ounce casserole. Mix remaining ingredients until crumbly; sprinkle over apple slices.

2. Microwave uncovered on High (100%) until apples are tender, 5 to 6 minutes. Serve warm with vanilla or cinnamon ice cream.

1 Serving: Calories 245 (Calories from Fat 110); Fat 12g (Saturated 7g); Cholesterol 30mg; Sodium 80mg; Carbohydrate 35g (Dietary Fiber 3g); Protein 2g • **% Daily Value:** Vitamin A 10%; Vitamin C 4%; Calcium 2%; Iron 6% • **Diet Exchanges:** 2 Fruit, 2 1/2 Fat

flaming pecan bananas

good 2 know For a dramatic dessert that's sure to impress a guest or any dinner partner, try these bananas drizzled with flaming rum. Be careful lighting the rum since it flames easily. If you prefer not to use rum and flame this dessert, just use a tablespoon of your favorite fruit juice to drizzle over the bananas. It's still a delicious dessert.

microwave 3 min

1 tablespoon butter or margarine

1 tablespoon honey

1/8 teaspoon ground nutmeg

1 firm banana, cut lengthwise into halves

1 tablespoon chopped pecans

1 tablespoon dark rum

1. Place butter in 12-ounce microwavable casserole. Microwave uncovered on High (100%) until melted, 25 to 30 seconds. Stir in honey and nutmeg. Place banana in honey mixture; roll to coat. Sprinkle with pecans. Microwave uncovered until hot, 1 to 2 minutes.

2. Place rum in 1-cup microwavable measure. Microwave uncovered on High (100%) just until warm, about 15 seconds. Pour rum into large metal serving spoon; carefully ignite rum in spoon and pour over bananas.

1 Serving: Calories 170 (Calories from Fat 80); Fat 9g (Saturated 4g); Cholesterol 15mg; Sodium 40mg; Carbohydrate 23g (Dietary Fiber 2g); Protein 1g • **% Daily Value:** Vitamin A 4%; Vitamin C 4%; Calcium 0%; Iron 2% • **Diet Exchanges:** 1 1/2 Fruit, 2 Fat

flaming pecan bananas

blueberry-pear crisps

good 2 know This delicious crisp is perfect in early autumn made with ripe pears and the last of the season's fresh blueberries.

prep 10 min • **bake** 30 min

1 small pear, peeled and coarsely chopped

1/2 cup fresh or frozen blueberries

2 tablespoons packed brown sugar

2 tablespoons whole wheat or all-purpose flour

1 tablespoon quick-cooking or regular oats

1/8 teaspoon apple pie spice or cinnamon

1 tablespoon butter or margarine (use only stick that has more than 65% vegetable oil)

Cream or ice cream, if desired

1. Heat oven to 375°. Grease two 6-ounce custard or soufflé cups.

2. Divide pear and blueberries between custard cups. Mix brown sugar, flour, oats and apple pie spice in small bowl. Cut in butter with pastry blender until mixture is crumbly; sprinkle over fruit.

3. Bake about 30 minutes or until topping is golden brown and pear is tender. Serve warm with cream or ice cream.

1 Serving: Calories 190 (Calories from Fat 55); Fat 6g (Saturated 4g); Cholesterol 15mg; Sodium 45mg; Carbohydrate 36g (Dietary Fiber 4g); Protein 2g • **% Daily Value:** Vitamin A 6%; Vitamin C 6%; Calcium 2%; Iron 4% • **Diet Exchanges:** 1/2 Starch, 2 Fruit, 1 Fat

fat

fruit cobblers

 good2know | Baking desserts in individual custard cups instead of a large baking dish means having just the right amount of dessert to share without having leftovers. The buttery crust bakes perfectly atop the cups of bubbling fruit.

prep 5 min • **bake** 18 min

1 cup pie filling (apple, peach, cherry or blueberry)

1/2 cup Original Bisquick

2 tablespoons milk

1 tablespoon sugar

1 teaspoon butter or margarine, softened

1. Heat oven to 400°. Divide pie filling between 2 ungreased 10-ounce custard cups.

2. Stir remaining ingredients until soft dough forms. Spoon half of dough onto pie filling in each custard cup. Sprinkle with additional sugar if desired.

3. Bake 15 to 18 minutes or until topping is light brown.

1 Serving: Calories 300 (Calories from Fat 55); Fat 6g (Saturated 2g); Cholesterol 5mg; Sodium 450mg; Carbohydrate 60g (Dietary Fiber 2g); Protein 3g • **% Daily Value:** Vitamin A 2%; Vitamin C 0%; Calcium 8%; Iron 6% • **Diet Exchanges:** 1 Starch, 3 Fruit, 1 Fat

individual coconut flans

good 2 know In the summer, you can refrigerate these flans for a cool and creamy tropical-tasting dessert.

prep 12 min • **steam** 12 min • **stand** 10 min

2 tablespoons flaked coconut

2 teaspoons caramel ice-cream topping

3/4 cup half-and-half

3 tablespoons sugar

1/4 teaspoon vanilla

Dash of ground allspice

1 egg

1 egg yolk

1. Place 1 tablespoon coconut in each of 2 ungreased 6-ounce custard cups. Drizzle 1 teaspoon ice-cream topping over each. Beat remaining ingredients with egg beater or wire whisk; pour into custard cups.

2. Place round baking rack or steamer rack in 10-inch skillet. Place custard cups on rack. Pour boiling water into skillet until it comes almost to the top of the rack. (Water should not touch custard cups.) Cover skillet and steam over medium heat 11 to 12 minutes or until knife inserted halfway between center and edge comes out clean. (Watch flans closely the last few minutes of steaming.)

3. Remove cups from skillet; let stand 10 minutes. Loosen sides of flans from cups, using sharp knife. Unmold flans onto dessert plates. Serve warm.

table for 2 Cinco de Mayo (May 5th) calls for a Mexican-inspired dinner. Start with vegetable sticks dipped in a mix of prepared salsa and sour cream; Black Bean–Pasta Cancun (page 82) for the main course; then this dreamy dessert for the finale to your Mexican fiesta!

1 Serving: Calories 300 (Calories from Fat 155); Fat 17g (Saturated 10g); Cholesterol 245mg; Sodium 110mg; Carbohydrate 30g (Dietary Fiber 0g); Protein 7g • **% Daily Value:** Vitamin A 14%; Vitamin C 0%; Calcium 12%; Iron 4% • **Diet Exchanges:** 2 Starch, 3 Fat

lemon curd parfaits

Rich and tangy lemon curd, a thick sauce almost with the consistency of a pudding, can be found in the jams and preserves section of the supermarket.

prep 8 min

1/2 cup lemon curd

2 tablespoons orange juice

1 cup whipped cream or frozen (thawed) whipped topping

8 chocolate wafer cookies

Raspberries, if desired

1. Mix lemon curd and orange juice in medium bowl. Fold in whipped cream. Coarsely crumble cookies; reserve 1 tablespoon crumbs.

2. Layer half of the lemon curd mixture, the cookie crumbs and remaining lemon curd mixture in 2 parfait glasses. Sprinkle with reserved crumbs and top with raspberries.

1 Serving: Calories 550 (Calories from Fat 250); Fat 28g (Saturated 16g); Cholesterol 90mg; Sodium 200mg; Carbohydrate 73g (Dietary Fiber 2g); Protein 4g • **% Daily Value:** Vitamin A 18%; Vitamin C 10%; Calcium 8%; Iron 8% • **Diet Exchanges:** Not Recommended

pineapple-lemon frost

Try this quick-to-make cooler on the hottest of summer days or after a spicy meal. Serve with a straw for sipping—this fruity refresher is guaranteed to cool you down!

prep 5 min

1 can (6 ounces) unsweetened pineapple juice

1/2 pint lemon sorbet (1 cup)

Mint leaves, if desired

Place pineapple juice and lemon sorbet in blender. Cover and blend until smooth. Pour into two 8-ounce glasses. Garnish with mint leaves. Serve immediately.

1 Serving: Calories 145 (Calories from Fat 0); Fat 0g (Saturated 0g); Cholesterol 0mg; Sodium 0mg; Carbohydrate 38g (Dietary Fiber 3g); Protein 1g • **% Daily Value:** Vitamin A 0%; Vitamin C 32%; Calcium 2%; Iron 2% • **Diet Exchanges:** 2 1/2 Fruit

pineapple-yogurt shortcake

good 2 know   If you don't have mace for these shortcakes, nutmeg has a similar sweet spiced flavor.

prep 5 min

1 can (8 ounces) crushed pineapple in juice, drained

1/2 cup vanilla or pineapple yogurt

1/8 teaspoon ground mace

2 sponge shortcake cups

2 tablespoons chopped toasted pecans

Mix pineapple, yogurt and mace; divide between shortcake cups. Sprinkle with pecans.

1 Serving: Calories 250 (Calories from Fat 65); Fat 7g (Saturated 1g); Cholesterol 40mg; Sodium 50mg; Carbohydrate 44g (Dietary Fiber 2g); Protein 5g • **% Daily Value:** Vitamin A 2%; Vitamin C 20%; Calcium 12%; Iron 4% • **Diet Exchanges:** 2 Starch, 1 Fruit,1 Fat

mango-lime cooler

good 2 know Frozen mango is terrific as well if you don't have fresh. It also saves you time, since the mango is already peeled and cut into cubes.

prep 5 min • *photograph on page 143*

1 ripe mango, peeled and cut into chunks

1/2 cup plain low-fat yogurt

1/2 cup low-fat (skim) milk

1 tablespoon honey

1 tablespoon lime juice

3 ice cubes, crushed

Place all ingredients except ice cubes in blender. Cover and blend on high speed about 15 seconds or until smooth. Add crushed ice and continue blending for 15 seconds or until blended.

1 Serving: Calories 160 (Calories from Fat 10); Fat 1g (Saturated 1g); Cholesterol 5mg; Sodium 80mg; Carbohydrate 34g (Dietary Fiber 2g); Protein 6g • **% Daily Value:** Vitamin A 18%; Vitamin C 52%; Calcium 20%; Iron 0% • **Diet Exchanges:** 2 Fruit, 1/2 Skim Milk

cran-apple crisp

good2know Some of the best apple varieties for baking are Braeburn, Fuji, Gala, Golden Delicious, Granny Smith, Greening, Jonagold and Rome. Try them all!

prep 5 min • bake 40 min

2 baking apples, cored and sliced

1 teaspoon lemon juice

1 tablespoon dried cranberries

1 tablespoon packed brown sugar

1 tablespoon butter or margarine, melted

4 gingersnaps, crushed

1. Heat oven to 375°. Spray 1-quart casserole with cooking spray.

2. Place apples in dish; sprinkle with lemon juice. Mix remaining ingredients until crumbly; sprinkle over apples. Cover with aluminum foil. Bake 30 to 40 minutes or until apples are tender.

1 Serving: Calories 210 (Calories from Fat 65); Fat 7g (Saturated 4g); Cholesterol 15mg; Sodium 120mg; Carbohydrate 39g (Dietary Fiber 3g); Protein 1g • **% Daily Value:** Vitamin A 6%; Vitamin C 4%; Calcium 2%; Iron 2% • **Diet Exchanges:** 1/2 Starch, 2 Fruit, 1 Fat

honey lime fruit salad

If you prefer to use fresh limes, 1 lime should yield about 2 tablespoons juice. Before juicing, you can grate a little bit of the lime peel to use for a flavorful garnish.

prep 5 min • **microwave** 40 sec

1 tablespoon lime juice

1 tablespoon honey

1/2 teaspoon cornstarch

1/8 teaspoon poppy seed

2 cups cut-up fresh fruit
(apples, oranges, grapes,
bananas or pears)

1. Mix lime juice, honey, cornstarch and poppy seed in 1-cup measure. Microwave uncovered on High (100%) until mixture thickens and boils, 30 to 40 seconds. Cool slightly.

2. Pour sauce over fruit in bowl; toss until fruit is glazed.

1 Serving: Calories 130 (Calories from Fat 0); Fat 0g (Saturated 0g); Cholesterol 0mg; Sodium 5mg; Carbohydrate 33g (Dietary Fiber 3g); Protein 1g • **% Daily Value:** Vitamin A 2%; Vitamin C 28%; Calcium 2%; Iron 2% • **Diet Exchanges:** 2 Fruit

honey lime fruit salad

raspberry yogurt pudding

You can have a different flavored pudding every night! How about lemon gelatin and lemon yogurt or cherry gelatin and cherry yogurt. Or you could combine different flavors like cherry gelatin and vanilla yogurt.

prep 5 min • **chill** 2 hr

3 tablespoons raspberry-
flavored gelatin
(1/2 three-ounce package)

3/4 cup boiling water

1 container (6 ounces)
raspberry yogurt

1. Stir together gelatin and water until gelatin is dissolved. Mix in yogurt.

2. Pour into two 6-ounce custard cups. Refrigerate until set, about 2 hours.

1 Serving: Calories 155 (Calories from Fat 10); Fat 1g (Saturated 0g); Cholesterol 5mg; Sodium 100mg; Carbohydrate 34g (Dietary Fiber 0g); Protein 5g • **% Daily Value:** Vitamin A 0%; Vitamin C 0%; Calcium 14%; Iron 0% • **Diet Exchanges:** 2 Fruit, 1/2 Skim Milk

chocolate-toffee torte

good know

You probably have most of the ingredients for this quick and easy dessert on hand in your refrigerator or freezer. To get cracking on this cake, freeze the candy bars for easier crushing or chopping.

prep 10 min

1/2 cup soft cream cheese

2 tablespoons powdered sugar

1 tablespoon Amaretto or 1/8 teaspoon almond extract

1 bar (1.4 ounces) chocolate-covered toffee candy

6 slices (about 1/4 inch each) frozen pound cake, thawed

1/4 cup fudge ice-cream topping

1. Mix cream cheese, powdered sugar and Amaretto. Place candy bar in small plastic bag; seal bag. Coarsely crush candy with rolling pin.

2. Spread cream cheese mixture over 4 of the cake slices. Reserve 1 teaspoon of the crushed candy. Sprinkle remaining candy over cream cheese. For each serving, stack 2 of the cream cheese-topped cake slices. Top each stack with 1 of the remaining cake slices. Top each stack with a dollop of ice-cream topping, spreading it slightly. Sprinkle with reserved candy.

1 Serving: Calories 520 (Calories from Fat 270); Fat 30g (Saturated 17g); Cholesterol 80mg; Sodium 320mg; Carbohydrate 57g (Dietary Fiber 2g); Protein 7g • **% Daily Value:** Vitamin A 16%; Vitamin C 0%; Calcium 10%; Iron 8% • **Diet Exchanges:** Not Recommended

fruit pizza

Here's a sweet and fruity idea that combines two homey favorites: pizza and cinnamon toast. It's great for dessert or even a quick breakfast.

prep 3 min • **bake** 10 min

1 flour or whole wheat flour tortilla (8 inches in diameter)

1/2 teaspoon sugar

Dash of cinnamon

2 tablespoons soft cream cheese

1/2 cup chopped fresh fruit (such as strawberries, grapes, peaches), well drained

1. Heat oven to 350°. Place tortilla on ungreased cookie sheet. Bake about 10 minutes or until crisp.

2. Meanwhile, mix sugar and cinnamon; reserve. Place hot tortilla on cutting board; spread cream cheese on tortilla. Sprinkle with sugar-cinnamon mixture; arrange fruit on top. Cut into 4 wedges; serve warm.

1 Serving: Calories 115 (Calories from Fat 45); Fat 5g (Saturated 3g); Cholesterol 10mg; Sodium 130mg; Carbohydrate 16g (Dietary Fiber 2g); Protein 3g • **% Daily Value:** Vitamin A 2%; Vitamin C 14%; Calcium 4%; Iron 4% • **Diet Exchanges:** 1/2 Starch, 1/2 Fruit, 1 Fat

fruit pizza

fruit trifle

good 2 know

You can purchase plain cupcakes, pound cake or sponge cake from the bakery section of the supermarket—then add just a few ingredients to turn it into a homemade trifle full of fresh fruit flavor.

prep 10 min

2 plain cupcakes or
pound cake slices

1 tablespoon currant jelly

6 strawberries

1 kiwifruit

1/4 cup frozen whipped
topping, thawed

1. Cut cupcakes into 1/2-inch cubes; divide between two 6-ounce custard cups. Place jelly in another 6-ounce custard cup and microwave uncovered on High (100%) until melted, 20 to 30 seconds; spoon over cake.

2. Slice 4 strawberries; peel and slice kiwifruit. Arrange sliced fruit on cake; spread with whipped topping. Garnish trifles with remaining strawberries.

1 Serving: Calories 145 (Calories from Fat 45); Fat 5g (Saturated 1g); Cholesterol 15mg; Sodium 100mg; Carbohydrate 26g (Dietary Fiber 3g); Protein 2g • **% Daily Value:** Vitamin A 0%; Vitamin C 96%; Calcium 4%; Iron 2% • **Diet Exchanges:** 1/2 Starch, 1 Fruit, 1 Fat

granola candy

These delicious snacks are great for days when you need to grab a bite to go—for an after-meal treat or even at breakfast.

prep 15 min • **chill** 10 min • **makes** 12 candies

1/2 cup low-fat granola

1/2 cup multigrain puffed cereal

2 tablespoons raisins or dried cranberries, if desired

1/2 cup miniature marshmallows

1 tablespoon honey

1 tablespoon peanut butter

1. Mix granola, puffed cereal and raisins in medium bowl. Heat remaining ingredients in small nonstick saucepan over low heat, stirring constantly, until marshmallows are melted. Immediately pour marshmallow mixture over cereal mixture; stir until coated.

2. With wet hands, divide into 1 1/2-inch balls. Place on waxed paper. Refrigerate at least 10 minutes.

table for **2**
Fill a picnic basket with an easy sandwich like Peppercorn Beef Pitas (page 34); a chilled veggie salad like Marinated Broccoli and Carrot Salad (page 133); and these chewy granola treats. Just tote along a thermos of lemonade and you're good to go!

1 Candy: Calories 40 (Calories from Fat 10); Fat 1g (Saturated 0g); Cholesterol 0mg; Sodium 15mg; Carbohydrate 7g (Dietary Fiber 0g); Protein 1g • **% Daily Value:** Vitamin A 0%; Vitamin C 0%; Calcium 0%; Iron 0% • **Diet Exchanges:** 1/2 Starch

helpful **nutrition** and **cooking** information

nutrition guidelines

We provide nutrition information for each recipe that includes calories, fat, cholesterol, sodium, carbohydrate, fiber and protein. Individual food choices can be based on this information.

Recommended intake for a daily diet of 2,000 calories as set by the Food and Drug Administration

Total Fat	Less than 65g
Saturated Fat	Less than 20g
Cholesterol	Less than 300mg
Sodium	Less than 2,400mg
Total Carbohydrate	300g
Dietary Fiber	25g

criteria used for calculating nutrition information

- The first ingredient was used wherever a choice is given (such as 1/3 cup sour cream or plain yogurt).

- The first ingredient amount was used wherever a range is given (such as 3- to 3-1/2–pound cut-up broiler-fryer chicken).

- The first serving number was used wherever a range is given (such as 4 to 6 servings).

- "If desired" ingredients and recipe variations were not included (such as sprinkle with brown sugar, if desired).

- Only the amount of a marinade or frying oil that is estimated to be absorbed by the food during preparation or cooking was calculated.

ingredients used in recipe testing and nutrition calculations

- Ingredients used for testing represent those that the majority of consumers use in their homes: large eggs, 2% milk, 80%-lean ground beef, canned ready-to-use chicken broth and vegetable oil spread containing not less than 65 percent fat.

- Fat-free, low-fat or low-sodium products were not used, unless otherwise indicated.

- Solid vegetable shortening (not butter, margarine, nonstick cooking sprays or vegetable oil spread as they can cause sticking problems) was used to grease pans, unless otherwise indicated.

equipment used in recipe testing

We use equipment for testing that the majority of consumers use in their homes. If a specific piece of equipment (such as a wire whisk) is necessary for recipe success, it is listed in the recipe.

- Cookware and bakeware without nonstick coatings were used, unless otherwise indicated.

- No dark-colored, black or insulated bakeware was used.

- When a pan is specified in a recipe, a metal pan was used; a baking dish or pie plate means ovenproof glass was used.

- An electric hand mixer was used for mixing only when mixer speeds are specified in the recipe directions. When a mixer speed is not given, a spoon or fork was used.

cooking terms glossary

Beat: Mix ingredients vigorously with spoon, fork, wire whisk, hand beater or electric mixer until smooth and uniform.

Boil: Heat liquid until bubbles rise continuously and break on the surface and steam is given off. For rolling boil, the bubbles form rapidly.

Chop: Cut into coarse or fine irregular pieces with a knife, food chopper, blender or food processor.

Cube: Cut into squares 1/2 inch or larger.

Dice: Cut into squares smaller than 1/2 inch.

Grate: Cut into tiny particles using small rough holes of grater (citrus peel or chocolate).

Grease: Rub the inside surface of a pan with shortening, using pastry brush, piece of waxed paper or paper towel, to prevent food from sticking during baking (as for some casseroles).

Julienne: Cut into thin, matchlike strips, using knife or food processor (vegetables, fruits, meats).

Mix: Combine ingredients in any way that distributes them evenly.

Sauté: Cook foods in hot oil or margarine over medium-high heat with frequent tossing and turning motion.

Shred: Cut into long thin pieces by rubbing food across the holes of a shredder, as for cheese, or by using a knife to slice very thinly, as for cabbage.

Simmer: Cook in liquid just below the boiling point on top of the stove; usually after reducing heat from a boil. Bubbles will rise slowly and break just below the surface.

Stir: Mix ingredients until uniform consistency. Stir once in a while for stirring occasionally, often for stirring frequently and continuously for stirring constantly.

Toss: Tumble ingredients (such as green salad) lightly with a lifting motion, usually to coat evenly or mix with another food.

metric conversion chart

Volume

U.S. Units	Canadian Metric	Australian Metric
1/4 teaspoon	1 mL	1 ml
1/2 teaspoon	2 mL	2 ml
1 teaspoon	5 mL	5 ml
1 tablespoon	15 mL	20 ml
1/4 cup	50 mL	60 ml
1/3 cup	75 mL	80 ml
1/2 cup	125 mL	125 ml
2/3 cup	150 mL	170 ml
3/4 cup	175 mL	190 ml
1 cup	250 mL	250 ml
1 quart	1 liter	1 liter
1 1/2 quarts	1.5 liters	1.5 liters
2 quarts	2 liters	2 liters
2 1/2 quarts	2.5 liters	2.5 liters
3 quarts	3 liters	3 liters
4 quarts	4 liters	4 liters

Measurements

Inches	Centimeters
1	2.5
2	5.0
3	7.5
4	10.0
5	12.5
6	15.0
7	17.5
8	20.5
9	23.0
10	25.5
11	28.0
12	30.5
13	33.0

Weight

U.S. Units	Canadian Metric	Australian Metric
1 ounce	30 grams	30 grams
2 ounces	55 grams	60 grams
3 ounces	85 grams	90 grams
4 ounces (1/4 pound)	115 grams	125 grams
8 ounces (1/2 pound)	225 grams	225 grams
16 ounces (1 pound)	455 grams	500 grams
1 pound	455 grams	1/2 kilogram

Temperatures

Fahrenheit	Celsius
32°	0°
212°	100°
250°	120°
275°	140°
300°	150°
325°	160°
350°	180°
375°	190°
400°	200°
425°	220°
450°	230°
475°	240°
500°	260°

Note: The recipes in this cookbook have not been developed or tested using metric measures. When converting recipes to metric, some variations in quality may be noted.

index

Complete your cookbook library
with these *Betty Crocker's* titles

Betty Crocker's A Passion for Pasta

Betty Crocker's Best Bread Machine Cookbook

Betty Crocker's Best Chicken Cookbook

Betty Crocker's Best Christmas Cookbook

Betty Crocker's Best of Baking

Betty Crocker's Best of Healthy and Hearty Cooking

Betty Crocker's Best-Loved Recipes

Betty Crocker's Bisquick® Cookbook

Betty Crocker's Bread Machine Cookbook

Betty Crocker's Cook It Quick

Betty Crocker's Cookbook, 9th Edition - *The* **BIG RED** *Cookbook*®

Betty Crocker's Cookbook, Bridal Edition

Betty Crocker's Cookie Book

Betty Crocker's Cooking and Coping with Cancer

Betty Crocker's Cooking Basics

Betty Crocker's Easy Slow Cooker Dinners

Betty Crocker's Eat and Lose Weight

Betty Crocker's Entertaining Basics

Betty Crocker's Flavors of Home

Betty Crocker's Good & Easy Cookbook

Betty Crocker's Great Grilling

Betty Crocker's Healthy New Choices

Betty Crocker's Indian Home Cooking

Betty Crocker's Italian Cooking

Betty Crocker's Kids Cook!

Betty Crocker's Kitchen Library

Betty Crocker's Low-Fat Low-Cholesterol Cooking Today

Betty Crocker's New Cake Decorating

Betty Crocker's New Chinese Cookbook

Betty Crocker's Picture Cook Book, Facsimile Edition

Betty Crocker's Slow Cooker Cookbook

Betty Crocker's Southwest Cooking

Betty Crocker's Vegetarian Cooking